D0909053

LOWER THAN ANGELS

LOWER THAN ANGELS

A Memoir Of War & Peace

W. W. WINDSTAFF

Illustrated & With
An Introduction By
STEPHEN LONGSTREET

enigma books
Silver Spring, Maryland

Published by:

Enigma Books
An Imprint of Bartleby Press
11141 Georgia Avenue
Silver Spring, MD 20902

Library of Congress Cataloging-in-Publication Data

Windstaff, W. W., 1898-1931.
　　Lower than angels : a memoir of war and peace / W. W.
　　Windstaff ; illustrated, and with an introduction, by Stephen
　　Longstreet.
　　　　p.　cm.
　　　　ISBN 0-910155-24-0 (hardcover) :
　　　　1. Windstaff, W. W., 1898-1931.　2. United States—Biography.
　　I. Longstreet, Stephen, 1907-　.　II. Title.
　　CT275.W58454A3　1993　　　　　　　　　　92-28335
　　　　　　　　　　　　　　　　　　　　　　　　　　　CIP

Manufactured in the United States of America

Contents

Introduction

The Windstaff memoirs have never before been published in their entirety; only a few short fragments have seen print. This is the first complete publication of the memoirs of an individual who wrote them under the pen name of W. W. Windstaff. He was a member of a well-known, socially prominent family: "I don't want my bare-assed bizarre hoots and hollers to embarrass them."

At seventeen, Windstaff had flown with the British as a fighter pilot in World War I and had been seriously wounded in air combat. He drifted about in the 1920s for some time in Paris and Greenwich Village and then settled in Rome.

Elliot Paul, co-editor of the Paris avant-garde magazine *transition*, who knew Windstaff, read the memoirs in manuscript and called them "the best and truest picture of the American expatriates in those cockeyed and wonderful years. And free of the romantic nonsense and boozy lies the survivors have written about the period. Here is, without the literary sweat or nostalgia rash, a truer picture than you'll find in Hemingway, Fitzgerald, or the inventions of Gertrude Stein. The best thing about Windstaff is that he had no itch for fame, no idea he was an *artiste*. He didn't give a good goddamn about publishing anything to make a reputation."

Windstaff created his memoirs almost by accident. In the spring of 1929 he was back in the United States attempting to get back into the good graces of his family, so as to get some money released to him from a family trust. He was also trying to cure himself of drinking. He was by that time a confirmed alcoholic. To pass the time, and shaky from the effects of not drinking, he began to write his memoirs.

I had known him in the past when I was a young painter. He told me he intended to publish his memoirs in a very small private edition of two dozen or so copies.

He was a marvelously vivid talker, but when I read the first few pages he had done of his manuscript, I found them leaden and concealing events behind a rather worn-out literary style. I suggested he present his life in the manner he spoke. Together, we expanded, edited, cut and added.

Windstaff planned to give copies as Christmas gifts for his friends. A small job printer began to set type and then things happened to affect the project. The great stock market crash of October 1929 took place; Windstaff could not get money from his family to pay the printer; and the printer refused to go on with the project.

Windstaff signed the copyright over to me in lieu of a payment he couldn't make for my editorial assistance. The last time I saw him, he tossed the manuscript at me: "It's all yours kid—fuck it."

In 1931, W. W. Windstaff was killed in an auto accident

while driving to Florida—he was forbidden to drive and had no license. I made no effort to publish the book, for in those unpermissive days, the language and certain details of the memoirs would have turned away any major publisher.

During the years I gave the text for a reading to various friends. I showed it to William Faulkner when we worked together on the screenplay of my novel *Stallion Road*. Faulkner, amused, said of it:

"For a non-writer W. W. Windstaff wrote a hell of a lot better than all those talkers and slogan makers that crowded the cafes of Europe between the wars, and looking for what? Windstaff had clearer answers than most: keep moving—stay alive."

Errol Flynn—I was writing his film "Silver River"— expressed a desire to star in a movie version of the Windstaff memoirs. He was, however, in the last stages of a long decline and no studio was interested.

And John Huston remembered:

"They were still talking about W. W. Windstaff, an extroverted American, of his times in Paris and Rome, when I took my own tours in Europe. It's clear he out-Hemingwayed Hemingway, and talked back to Gertrude Stein: *That* took balls."

I did slip a little of the Windstaff material into a novel, and when I later wrote two genre histories—of the planes and fliers of World War I, *The Canvas Falcons*, and of Americans in *We All Went to Paris*—I quoted from the memoirs, although editors changed some of the language, it being "rather gamey."

The fragments created great interest, and several publishers suggested the publication of the entire Windstaff memoirs. I delayed because there was the editorial problem of getting a clean copy from the messed-up typescript that had survived the years, written over in two kinds of colored inks, pencil markings with inserts and rubbings, and smears by both of us.

In 1974 a mid-Western publisher was ready to issue the memoirs—but that unlucky editor went out to shovel snow and died on the spot.

The present publisher discovered the only surviving full text in the special Longstreet Collection at the Mugar Memorial Library at Boston University.

The illustrations are from my Paris and New York sketchbooks of the mid-1920s. The war sketches are not imaginary. They were produced from studying a collection of war photographs Windstaff had acquired. We worked with them to catch what he felt was the proper atmosphere and detail.

One thing should be noted about Windstaff's memoirs. Windstaff is writing of another era where terms used to identify certain minorities are no longer in style. He was not a bigot in his picture of the world as he lived it. But he does use now rejected terms like *darkie* and *wop*, *nance* and *pansy*—among others—as if they were the common accepted natural talk of his day, which they were.

Stephen Longstreet

Miradero Road, California, 1992

Not So Innocent Days

Me and Mine

I was raised by my grandfather, who gave me a great deal of advice when I was growing up. Of that advice, I only remember two things: "Never pay for getting into bed with a woman if you can avoid it," and, "Your mother's family always treated money as if it were snowflakes. So always count your change."

My grandfather's family were God-fearing greedy bastards with good church-going records, and the gravestones to prove it in a graveyard I still visit. New England stock—smart, given to education, mince pie once a year (how I hated it), and the comforts of good rich living. After a few generations of rational frugality, they liked caviar, private railroad cars, the best horses, and the first autocars. The family mills and machine plants paid a solid flow of dividends; the family supported missions to get Hottentots to cover their twats and fuck indoors. My family

3

built libraries, gave fountains to village squares. The family also had a few bones in the closet; an uncle who murdered his wife and her lover ("Not guilty"); a roaring pansy who sucked Boston cocks in public toilets; a great aunt who was caught cheating at cards at the Antlers out in Denver. I leave out the tics, the hopeless rashes, a peeping Tom or two.

If there ever was a writer, painter, poet, or violin player among us for the last two hundred years, it was kept a secret. My mother's people, boisterous boors, were bare-assed Southern gentry who were ruined, they claimed, by the War Between the States, but, actually, they didn't even own the slaves on the decaying plantations they had neglected for a hundred years—they were mortgaged to a New Orleans bank. There was a strain of feeble-mindedness, a genius for poker, dancing, fox hunting, and stories of a couple of family idiots chained up in the attic. What I know of my mother—she and my father died of some quick-killing fever in Louisiana while visiting the family sugar interests when I was seven—she seemed pretty much a bit off her nut, or just simple. Very beautiful, leaving boxes of Sherry chocolates around with her teeth marks on those candies she had bitten into, didn't like, discarded. For some dumb reason, when I think of her, I think of potted fuchsia and croquet mallets.

My grandfather's side of the family had all the money and about sixty relatives to sit on it, compound it, invest it. And spend large sums for things like church work, horses, cunt, and society balls in season. I had several uncles who were always having women troubles—"Man's overuse of nature," my grandfather called it—and paying for it. This annoyed my grandfather, as he didn't believe in paying for it. He'd take his own hardons, and he was over seventy at the time, to whack away on the high-yellow housekeeper. She was up on the third floor of the big Victorian house where we all lived. He'd come down slacked out, breathing hard. I remember when I was sixteen, after one of his trips upstairs, him saying, "I do it to save your grandmother's back."

I had a damn happy childhood, no lamentable ingratitudes. As I always thought *David Copperfield* was the story of a prig and a shitheel, if I ever read of one, I'm not going to go too much into details of me growing up. I ate a lot, was very neat, liked good clothes, ran wild around the place, raised a ruckus. Got walloped without mercy by my grandmother—my grandfather never struck me. There were still woods and streams around the middle-sized town of the Eastern seaboard—dominated by the family factories and machinery works. I suppose it was all some horrendous inconsistency—grim slums and green fields, shithouses and Greek gazebos. I rode horses—the stables weren't made into garages until 1910 when I was twelve and my grandfather got his first cars. A Simplex, a Templar, and finally a huge Pierce-Arrow "long as a tapeworm," someone said.

Life was better before the Great War if you had enough money and moxie, *and* if you ached for a great chunk of hedonism, it was there—just pay the bill. Even the mill and factory workers got cockeyed drunk every Saturday night, beat their wives, raised merry hell. They once busted our French windows during a strike. My grandfather let them organize unions in 1913, then bribed the union leaders to sell out the workers and speed up production.

I had two special friends, Chunky—fat, short, apple-faced, whose family owned a bicycle shop, and whose father had been a champion wheeler, a *Police Gazette* medal winner back in the days of the high-wheel bike. My other buddy was John B——, whose father was a minister, a hell-fire sinner grabber. A white-haired old Bible pounder who'd preach hell and damnation on all non-Baptists, Catholics, and Democrats. He raised pigs, slaughtered them himself, and won prizes at flower shows. John's ass was usually sore from the beatings he got from his old man from time to time for smoking coffin nails, smelling of beer, neglecting his chores.

We three—Chunky, John, and I—were the real American stuff you read of in the books of Earl Reed Silvers, the Lawrenceville stories, Ralph Henry Barbour (I hope I'm remembering the names right). We got drugged on the Rover Boys, Nick Carter, the first Tom Swifts. We smoked Piedmont, stole family whiskey—didn't like it; jerked off together in the tack room of the coach house. We were also fine fishermen, became expert rod and reel users. We bicycled thirty, forty miles a day, carrying packets of fish cakes, frankfurters which, in those days, were solid meat and garlicky. We roasted mickies in open field fires and ate the hot potatoes and got the charcoal all over us. We'd go scorching through the towns and yell at the girls in bravura spasms of hot-nuts romanticism. Late at night we'd pedal back home lighting our gas bike lamps, sometimes getting caught in some summer night rain, feeling unique and leg-tired and somehow pleased with ourselves.

We'd steal some—no passionate commitment to it like the poor, nothing fancy and nothing to hock in a pawnshop. I didn't get much of an allowance, but I could ask for and get most things like barbells, a small skiff, field glasses, tools to dissect frogs and stuff an owl.

We bullshitted a lot—telling of touching pussy, drinking bourbon—with the other boys at Donkin's Drug Store, sipping dopes and asking old man Donkin to pile the banana splits taller, screw the cost, we'd go as high as fifteen or twenty cents. The town whores hung out at the River Hotel. We dreamed of more than casual dalliance but were scared of the clap and the ole rale.

Flying was how we three differed from the usual town kids. We had this big ledger from some discarded bookkeeping system at the mills. In it we pasted everything we could find on flying. But mostly we thought and talked of girls as our first pubic hair thickened.

Our town was on a trolley line operating along the upper river towns—linking villages, cities, the beer gardens, and picnic grounds. John and I were interested in girls and hung around the drug store where a girl named Shirl, who had a sister named Mona, worked at the beauty counter. There was a display of empty cartons on a wall and Shirl not only sold, demonstrated, but she also wore the products a little too strongly, garishly. She was what they called in the town a strawberry blonde, about nineteen years of age—and to me at fifteen, very beautiful and plump. Mona, a year older, was my favorite.

John and I would put on our bicycle caps and ride down toward Donkin's Corner Drug Store. A wide, deep shop, painted yellow, each window containing a huge glass jar of colored water, red in the right, blue-green in the left, dead flies, paper roses. Inside were two walls full of dark cases of strange drugs, bottles, and crutches, and plasters, and the Trojan condoms close by in a drawer. Mr. Donkin had posters—I still remember the names: Carboline For the Hair, Wizard, Neuralgia oil; Brown's Vegetable Tonic for Female Weakness, Disorders, Leucorrhea; Drink Moxie; Fatima cigarettes. In the back was a counter of black mottled marble and an examining room behind a display of Celery Malt Compound. Here Mr. Donkin, rosy-cheeked behind a sheriff's moustache, in a checked vest, served and prepared drugs and potions. Here he fitted trusses and corrective girdles for men, explained prostates, bad breath, clap symptoms, and drunk cures; while Shirl did a milder version for the women and praised hair color and a breast food ("Pat on hard for half an hour"), corrective corsets and rubber stockings. Damn it, we don't have 1913 drug stores anymore. To the right of the door was an ancient chipped stone soda fountain with a machine that combined marble dust and acid in its copper guts to produce a carbonized soda water that hissed from a swan's neck dispenser and tasted of frogs and sand.

Shirl sat here waiting for the trade, adjusting her reddish blonde hair. Tits outlined against a background of slightly spoiled fruit in a cut-glass bowl, bruised bananas, grapes.

"How about a date Shirl," I asked. "You and John. Me and Mona?"

"Kerist," she said in a sad voice. "Kids, summer kids."

She came around from behind the counter and we saw she was wearing what was called a Rainy Daisy skirt.

"How about tonight? Meet us on the trolley."

"The six-thirty one. Be on it. We'll get along ginger-peachy."

I suppose one always remembers one's first big approach to sex.

I Lose My Cherry

At six-thirty, John and I got on the river trolley at Dutchman's Corner. It was a warm night, sticky fragrant, the open cars cool, the wide straw seats comfortable. The motorman clanged his bell as he worked his power and brake handles. The trolley was usually half filled with people going out toward the roadhouses and beer gardens at the end of the line. At the next stop, Shirl and Mona got on and joined us. Jesus! I felt mature and horny, worldly wise, pawing the ground.

The motorman, after twenty minutes, half-turned as he spun his brake crank and cut off the power. "Gottlieb's Gardens."

About half the trolley passengers piled off—pinching, hugging, and laughing—among the ferns and gravel walks under a canopy topped by a row of electric lamps that spelled out: GOTTLIEB'S *ALT WIEN* BEER GARDENS.

The sound of the German zithers in the gardens playing Victor Herbert reached us. We each grabbed a girl and ran. We came to a gaslit clearing with a wooden floor and tables in the open under grape arbors attached to an Austrian-Swiss-chalet style of house. In one corner, red-coated bandsmen were playing what my music teacher called *aschlamperei*. John let out an Indian cry. "Wah-hoo!" A waiter rushed forward to quiet us.

"Pig knuckles and large lager beers. Rhine wine for the ladies."

The night wind came in over the flaring gaslights and stirred the checked tablecloths and was cool on my hot face. My underwear felt tight. Truth was we hadn't seen much of beer gardens, John and I. We sweated and affected a lazy sky's-the-limit air; one had to appear worldly.

The Rhine wine and seltzer and beers came. I already had a hand on Mona's soft thigh.

Papa Gottlieb, fat, smiling, a cheerful man, came over to us— he knew my grandfather.

"Mr. Gottlieb, your musicians play good and loud."

John said, "Let's dance."

It seemed a good idea after a huge schooner of strong 1913 beer. And Mona was slapping away my hand and smiling with her mouth open.

"Oh you," she kept saying, "oh you—fresh!"

It was deceptive stuff, the lager beer served at Pop Gottlieb's *Alt Wien*—a beer dark and musty, easy to swallow. On the third round John, after a dance, was leaning on his elbows, staring into the plates of pig's knuckles and calf's-head jelly. I was kissing Mona on the dance floor, hands cupped on her buttocks— living sofa cushions.

I got drunk that night for the first time in my life—I also had my first full sexual experience.

"Mary and Joseph," Mona said. "Just *look* at you."

There I was lying on the grassy river bank, my head gay with the sensation of floating. I was drunk. I had come twice while rolling all over Mona. I knew *that*. It was a pleasant state, full of some ribald amusement. All the world rose in colored rings and the ground was like breathing under me, with its arms around my neck. I turned and saw in the moonlight (like a song cover) the face of Mona. Willful and erratic twitching came back to me. My dick hung limp.

"Um—um."

"You fresh boy."

She bent and kissed me pushing her tongue forward, and I smelled girl, her body, and I felt her arms and then went in under her unbuttoned blouse. Her breasts were soft and warm, like unbaked bread dough. Yes, it's sweet and fascinating, this sex, I decided. No wonder men killed for it, women got paid for it.

"Where are the others?"

Mona's choked laughter sounded. "Oh, we lost them half an hour ago. I mean just working for a living don't mean I'm no lady, does it, sweetie? I'm not a bum."

I tried to sit up and saw Mona's pale yellow skirt way above her knees, the black stockings, garter clasps, the white thighs ending in the inevitable center of the pubic patch—perhaps it was "the labyrinth of deception and desire" the Bishop at the prep school preached against. A cunt crisp, crinkly, humid, alive. She giggled. "I must get home now or Pop will skin Shirl and me alive."

I sat up and buttoned my open shirt, my fly, found my jacket crumpled under Mona's ass. She wriggled off it and I put it on. She rearranged herself and stood up by my side trying to rehook herself. Everything was hooks, buttons, and bows then.

John and Shirl appeared from down the path, arms around each other. "Let's run or we'll miss the last trolley." The girls were tucking in their clothes and in amused confidence adjusting their high-piled hair.

I felt it was all pure promise of a wonderful life ahead—the four of us sitting in the open trolley, letting the cool night air blow on us. Mona smiling, cocky; as if she had solved the riddle of the universe by spreading her legs.

I looked around us. What if some of grandfather's friends should see us, I thought, with rumpled girls smelling of intimate relations. Most likely they'd report it—your young grandson, loose women, holding hands, reeking of beer, on the late trolley. But there was only an elderly Polish woman huddled in her shawl and holding a basket of eggs, and two darkies, lovers, making laughing sounds, feeding each other saltwater taffy.

The girls lived two stations before Dutchman's Corner. We saw them home to a tall, neglected brick house deep in uncut grass. Mona clung to my mouth at good-bye. "Come to the store, any excuse."

They were gone in a flash of skirts and a wave of white arms. John and I walked slowly away, our heads dreadfully aching.

I said, "John, you wondering if we are hell damned or started on a long life of dissipations?"

"Who cares?"

We came in sight of John's folks' white frame house and we went around to the back. At the old yard pump, we gulped up tepid water, and both vomited it up with, we hoped, most of the beer and delicatessen trimmings. Weak and shaky, John wiped his mouth on what he thought was his handkerchief. I saw the lace on it, a big-crotched female garment. We shoved the drawers into the yard incinerator.

It's all so clear. I can remember almost everything we said—a lot of what we did—all the times we took them out. They were simple girls, hardly educated—we were not their first affairs. At first they demanded little of us but our cocks and sodas. Mona liked a gin, but at our ages, it was hard to order.

We were "the rich kids," even if John was the son of a penniless church official—and I got only a dollar or so a week—but I had charge accounts, and stole a little. We were not at all like the factory apprentices, hired hands, store clerks from among whom they'd find a husband. It was a time of every boy having a chance, but girls were pretty much either wage earners or genteel decor—they had little chance to better themselves unless they broke out of their class by whoring or marriage.

I remember that for several weeks that long summer, some nights John and I slid out of our houses after dinner, put on our caps, and went down to the little park by the river. There was a refreshment stand with yellow gaslights, a dark green walk with splintered benches and not enough lamps glaring down on you and the shrubbery. It was a place of stray dogs, old men with no children left sleeping away their remaining years. And lovers came to merge with the underbrush and find nests for themselves, to whisper and hug and grab at the lovemaking tools of men and women. It was summer courtship: quick unbuttoning to whatever degree emotions drove. There was a kind of blood-heating night ripeness in the park, in damp grass.

Shirl and Mona, my girl (she was a sales clerk at the Notion Store) had little giggles, a crackling outburst of amusement at all the playful strength in us, our sex-crazy limbs. We had no idea of the refinements of sensual play beyond a few simple clownish sucking experiments which we blamed on the dirty French.

Mona one night said as we reclined in the park bushes, arms around each other, exposed to a moon low enough to bite. "You don't act serious."

"You're fine, Mona, just fine."

She nibbled on my ear, "Aren't we fighting just like a regular married couple?"

I decided not to talk of married couples.

All that summer we had a lot of what married couples did. John said we were just adolescents trying ourselves out all the way and accepting with an interest life and love as it was along the river, in the town. We had decided, John and myself—that the beginning of it all had delighted and surprised us. And now we wondered if we wanted it sustained at such a pace. Almost scientifically, John considered it as a domestic trap for a couple of fifteen-year-olds. "They all want to get married. It's nature's trap. We'll end up pushing baby carriages full of wet shitty kids. We've got to withdraw, literally."

My damn problem was I couldn't feel any true love in it—like in the novels I read. We would screw, Mona, me, the two of us, by the river bank nights with the other gash lovers paired off along the paths and river grass. The girls were not given to much mental effort, but they were willing and soft. We went on hayrides, watermelon picnics, boat rides. It settled into a pattern, and John said towns like ours can force issues.

We did not break up at once—no quarrel. We went two or three times a week to the river park to screw. We were, in Mona's words, "sweeties." It was accepted, a permanent relationship, at least to them.

We drank too much of the local booze, a potent applejack. Shaking as if with fever, leaving the girls at their trolley stop, we'd go to our back porch.

"Feel as if my skull is cracking open."

"Did you cat up anything?" John would ask.

"Doesn't help."

"No."

We sat—young, introspective—and felt in the nadir of our strength. Life, a whacky stupendous dream at fifteen *if* one had the courage to reach. I had this feeling of the impermanence of everything but what I felt in my groin. We sat in a kind of drunken stupor. "Oh that beer." I helped John up, we clung to each other. He put a finger on his lips. "Sh, sh!"

"Sh," I answered, and tried to pick John's hat off the ground and failed.

We stood, unbuttoned and emptied bladders with pleasure in the old hollyhock bed.

The stairs inside my grandfather's house were an ordeal, but at last I was in bed, shoes, collar, and tie off. It was the best

I could do. The scent of girls and our lovemaking was hard to get rid of, but I didn't mind. I yawned, remembering a line of a street corner preacher: "The flesh lusteth contrary to the spirit."

It was a hell of a busy summer. But our equal interest was still in flying, in the aeroplane.

What Does a Boy Want?

Our scrapbook filled with Wright biplanes, the Curtiss *Golden Flier*, what Blériot was doing, and the Voisons. We saved magazine stories, newspaper pictures, and even cut up publications in the town's Carnegie Free Public Library to add items to our ledger's contents. We were all going to be fliers and better the record of Curtiss the year he flew his *Golden Bug* four-cylinder job for nearly twenty-five miles at thirty miles an hour and won the *Scientific American* cup. We talked of Farman, Dela-grange, St. Dumont, the way most of the kids talked of the Yan-kees and Jack Johnson.

In 1913, Charlie G—— out at the meadows on the pike, had built himself a plane, a modified two seater, a copy of the 1911 Blériot. Charlie—no front teeth and a stutter—was taking people up for a ride at two dollars for five minutes. His plane had bicycle wheels, a cranky rotary engine gotten from France.

I sold my father's gold hunter's watch with scenes in relief on it of some Greek goddess being chased by hairy men with goat's legs. I sold it for enough to take flying lessons from Charlie, and even give Chunky and John a round in the air. The damn engine was a Gnome and the crankshaft and the propeller rotated together. The stink of the castor oil Charlie used to lubricate the thing made me remember old bellyaches, fever in a spinning room, and one of the facetious hired girls of my grandmother's rushing the chamber pot.

I flew. God, the punch-in-the-nose wonder of it. Never solo. Charlie had his life's savings invested in his aeroplane and he planned to take it out to the fairgrounds all through the country east of the Mississippi in 1915 for exhibition flying.

The Great War of course added a lot of clippings and pictures to our ledger's aeroplane collection. We had stopped calling them flying machines. There really wasn't much information yet of what the actual flying and fighting in the skies was like. One report said enemy fliers threw rocks at each other. We three were finishing high school, fucking the factory girls nights down by the canal, and trying to play football, wet kiss the high-school beauties at the Y dances, church suppers, and at the annual high-school prom. We were in that late teen-age state of uncertainty; were we colts or stallions?

After one dance we smoked some of my grandfather's cigars, Rafael Gonzales and Hoyo de Montereys, I had lifted from his teak humidor and we got sick. Also I broke my nose for the first time landing Charlie's plane at too sharp an angle. It improved my looks, I think; I told my grandfather I had fallen off my bicycle, and he gave a long thin fart, like a note on a flute, and said, "We used to fall off horses."

I was supposed to enter Harvard in the fall of 1915. The family having all been Yale men, but my grandfather had gone sour on Yale; something to do about the Yale Skull and Bones crowd getting him drunk for three days and having a burlesque girl from the old Howard Theater going down on him before the assembled brothers. I didn't feel any need for Harvard myself. Christ, all John and Chunky could think of was the romance of flying for the Allies, wearing those tight, well-cut flying tunics, the polished boots, carrying a swagger stick, and getting in bed with beautiful English society women or complaisant French countesses serving as Red Cross nurses.

In your early teens, your mind is randy all the time, but no one really writes the truth about boys. It's a time you have this strange idea of ideal women in fancy peignoirs, all submissive but passionate and mystical. Not at all like the aunts and nieces, the mill girls or the dancing school partners whose still-present baby fat you'd grope at, or try to dance your fingers above the elastic garters holding up their white stockings. It's a terrible yet wonderful time of a trembling in the loins and a feeling sin has you by the ass.

I don't know why no one has ever set down in books how a boy really grows up and how his nuts drive him in fantasy. But I guess we have to keep up the lies, hide what life really is like. Just as nobody had ever really told the truth about war. Not in my boy's world anyway. And so there I was—unglaublich— all glands, fairy tales, and wet dreams. I had images of myself, with just a slight wound, a nice clean bandage around my brow, leaning on a cane and maybe dressed in the horizon blue uniform of the French. My big problem was—did I look best in Bond Street cut of the English RFC or in the marvelous azure of the French officers and their cheesebox hats?

In March of 1915 I was seventeen and I told my grandfather I was going to Canada to enlist in the air force. I must say the old coot didn't rant or rave. He just sniffed the end of his burning double claro cigar and broke wind lightly; he was having digestive problems as he grew older and, when facing a problem, farted. "Jesus, you're still wet-nosed and can't see the world is actually going to hell in a hack. But go ahead, only tell your grandmother you're going up there for salmon fishing. Jesus, I was only fifteen when they sent me out to Kansas, and it was Bloody Kansas then, to go buy hides to be made into machine leather belting. We used steam then in the mills. One big engine for each plant. Kansas, it made me a human adult. I killed a man when I was sixteen. It was in Lawrence and—"

I didn't give a shit about my grandfather's killing. I had heard the story at least fifty times, how my grandfather had or had not killed the man, or two men. In a livery stable in a jerkwater Kansas town a long time ago.

Canada! John, of course, couldn't get his father the minister to agree for him to go to war. But he'd go anyway. Chunky would join us later. John's father was a man of peace. He thought war an abomination and tried to flog the idea of brotherly love, universal peace; into the asses of his nine kids with a leather razor strop. Chunky's father was a widower, drinking hard and playing poker with fellow Elks and the firehouse crew at Station B, also the political gang stealing the county blind, as the wartime prosperity was making all the mill and factory owners rich. Chunky's father didn't care what Chunky did. He had expanded into steel plate selling on commission.

So we would go off to the Great War, ignorant, callow, laughing and scratching, having no goddamn idea of the reality of things. Or what life was really all about. What misery people lived in—how mean man was. How full of shit most politicians were. We didn't see how the world was living on lies and would go on living that way. But in 1915 no one could tell us anything.

A Personal Battle

C ame the crazy exciting day John and I entrained for Canada with our long underwear, money belts, lice powder, two dozen condoms, and two ivory-handled .45 Colts, a gift from my grandfather. We were off for the war "over there" and bursting with illusions. Later John said we had screwed our youth. I always thought our youth had screwed us, made us opaque to reality. But that came later.

We found that the prosaic system of air training in Canada was to shove everybody into a fast training course at a private flying school with Sopwith Pups and kill off all the awkward chaps. It was simplification—toward the essence of war, speedy and obvious. John and I were scared pissless by the speed, relatively, of those small wire- and canvas-trainers, but we caught the hang of it. Brooks Brothers made us uniforms; we learned to carry a swagger stick. And once every two weeks, horny as mink, we hired a car for a trip to Toronto where we ate, drank, went to bed with local cunt, and later dreamed we were falling in flames. We made friends with a Canadian named Harry Glenn Moore, and saw him mashed to jelly when he ran his trainer into a hillside.

One rainy sleety day Chunky showed up at our training base with an alligator bag and his guitar. We hugged like lovers, drank warm beer, and sang our alma mater song.

"This is it, fellas—this is it!" Chunky said.

"How'd you wrangle it?" John asked. John was too tall, too thin, and asked too many questions.

"Got the old man's sales agent in England to write a letter."

It was not what I would call detailed and too expert training. But then they didn't know too much yet about their planes and air fighting. We took gunnery practice. Firing the machine guns on the ground, learning all the lousy tricks they had of jamming. How to reload quickly. We also had gunnery from the air, firing practice rounds at circles painted on the ground. And some fatal crashes. "Weeds out the unfit chaps." One boy, he got up middle of the night, after a jolly evening, drinks and songs, and blew off his head in the latrines.

Soon the rumors were we were going over to England for final flying lessons. There was leave home for some of us. Chunky and I went home for a week. John stayed on, as he was cozying some Canadian widow for her cooking and her bed. He also didn't want to face his father the minister.

I had a project in mind for my leave. I wanted to get Miss L——, my high-school art teacher, into bed. At seventeen such a project can take on, inside you, the whole goddamn fury of the entire Trojan War. She was not young—but lusciously mature—at least twenty-eight. Marvelously built. We used to kiss each other after class when I helped cut the Watman board into small sizes. Hug and whisper and laugh. She would grab her lower lip with her teeth and say, "God, god, you're *so* young, *so* young." Then Miss L——, she'd call out my name and I'd get my hand up her leg, close to pussy—but not too near—and she'd rub my fly, she panting a bit. But that was it. Miss L—— had this reputation of cock teasing the older boy students, and permitting a little groping and very wet kissing after class when they were helping her with the art supplies. But *that* was it.

I figured here I was, a hero now, on leave. Going out to die for her and civilization. For me she would spread her legs, hug me to her mature breasts. There is great confidence when you're a hot-nuts puppy, with an idea that no sensible girl would resist you. If she did, there was certainly something wrong with her, the freak.

My grandparents said I looked too thin, and my grandfather asked if the Canadian dark ale was as good as it used to be in 1905.

I called Miss L—— on the phone and told her I was back on leave before facing "The Great Adventure," and had seen some murals in Canada I'd like to talk about, and say goodbye—"One doesn't know the future does one, Miss L——?" (I never called her anything but Miss L——.)

She said come on over after dinner. She had some Burne-Jones reproductions she had just gotten. I said "good-o" like an Australian flier in Canada said it. I didn't wear my uniform. I figured to take it off to get into bed with Miss L—— would be too much to unbuckle, tight boots to drop off. No, a neat loose tweed suit, Arrow collar shirt, knitted tie.

The house of Miss L——'s grandfather, old Waldo L——, was of simple gray clapboard set back from a picket fence; it even had wormy roses, neglected honeysuckles. Waldo L—— had been a sergeant with Sickles' Brigade. He missed Gettysburg, he always said, because of a blister on his heel that became infected. Miss L——'s grandfather was a small man with yellowish soiled-looking hair, two small blue eyes beady as a doll's. He marched once a year on Decoration Day in the GAR section of the parade, a hickory cane on his shoulder, his bronze medals and faded ribbons on his narrow chest.

He sat in a rocker on the front porch, one cheek deformed by a chaw of tobacco, full of diseases but still above ground.

"Evening Captain L——."

The old man turned his head to shout through the screen door, "Fella out here for you."

I turned slightly away, feeling it impolite to show the old man my erection. I thought of the multiplication tables to deflate myself. Miss L——'s voice floated out through the screen door. "Come in, I'm in the back parlor."

I walked through the hall hung with a batik curtain we had made in art class the year before. Miss L—— was standing under the hiss of a gas globe; she looked marvelously healthy. In a pale green silk skirt, a crisp apple-yellow linen shirtwaist, and a wide black patent-leather belt around her waistline, reddish chestnut hair combed up with two curls resting on her fine white neck. I felt the imminence of a God who made such flesh. I was a believer.

"You look great, Miss L——"

"You're going to war?"

We sat down on a bamboo sofa with red velvet cushions. She had a personal odor—a woman odor under the scent and bath powder—slightly menstrual, I think, very pleasing to me. The little back parlor was Miss L——'s studio—she called it "mon atelier." There was a plaster reproduction of Hermes by Praxiteles with a tin fig leaf over his cock and balls.

"So!" Thigh, knee, leg, foot nearly touched me as I pressed close.

"We're getting a new lantern-slide projector. I'm showing color slides next sessions of Rembrandt's paintings and etchings."

I pressed closer.

"Behave. You're a guest in my grandfather's house."

We were both listening to her grandfather rock himself on

the front porch. Miss L—— got up, projecting front and back, in the round, and went to the small gramophone. She had the most magnificent ass, I decided, under that soft pleated skirt. She picked up two records. "You heard the new Victor Herbert? All the knuts sing it."

I went up behind her and I put my arms around her breasts and kissed the back of her neck. She had, under the skin cream, that special odor of girl sweat.

"Please. Unh-*unh!*"

"Miss L——, please," I answered. "You're here and I'm unable to stay off you."

She laughed, and I got my fingers on her breasts. They became alerted to my mangling. She leaned her head back and inhaled sharply a suck of air. Her voice broke. "You *must* behave. You're a man now, going to war."

"I'll behave like a man." Her nipples rose to my fingertips, and she half turned and we kissed as we had kissed I suppose a hundred times or more in the last two years. A slow pressure, a moistening of our lips, a forcing of our mouths to open, a bit of slow play of our tongues. We were no goddamn fumbling bumpkins about kissing.

There was the creak of old floorboards in the front hall. We held our breaths. The old man was going upstairs to rock himself in his room. Moths bumbled against the window screen behind the pulled drapes.

Miss L—— shook herself free of me, put a record on the gramophone and wound up its spring with a firm hand and arm action. Tinny music as if played at a distance across a lake, sent out sugary notes. I took out my grandfather's silver-bound pocket flask. It contained some of his best brandy, which he knew wasn't really Napoleon—that no longer existed—but it was good enough. Tonight I had added some Jersey lightning. Two little silver cups screwed on over the flask stopper, and I filled both with the doctored brandy while Miss L—— adjusted the gramophone sound

by moving the buttercup-shaped horn. I felt no nervous insta-
bility. This was our first catch-as-catch-can match outside the
after-school classroom messing around.

I handed her a little silver cup. "Damn it, Miss L——, you
look just great."

"Thank you."

"And to what has brought us this close, art!"

"To art."

The music ground on, we sipped the brandy, I eyed Miss
L—— expertly; a general viewing the battlefield before engaging,
wondering at the use of a sudden attack or the advantage of
flanking, the covering up of a sneaking approach in secret, allow-
ing for circumstances—like an old man rocking upstairs.

She finished her drink quickly and I refilled all around. She
gave me the Mona Lisa smile from the copy on the wall and
held out her arms and I dived in between them and we did a
slow waltz around the little room pressed close, legs locked. I
bit her neck lightly and she said softly, "Bite my ear. Don't leave
any bruises."

"Omm."

When the music stopped, I reset the playing needle to the
beginning, not letting go of Miss L——; I had my right leg
forward—like the pose of the Greek statue tossing a discus—
between her thighs and was gently rocking, wondering at a bold
frontal assault. I remembered General Grant and the sliding attack
around Lee's forces in Virginia, always keeping Lee off balance.

Miss L—— had her eyes half closed and we finished our second brandy, swayed to the tacky ragtime music which seemed
to help us both. I put my hands over her wonderful buttocks
and leaned her back over the dictionary stand and its Webster
Unabridged. She gave off a wonderful body heat. I was pleased
I was alive and functioning, and so determined to qualify her
for the glory of my manhood and for her own pleasure.

We didn't play any more records. Miss L—— modestly low-

ered the glare of the gas globe on the wall. We sat down on the
sofa on the limp Turkish harem cushions. We had our third
brandy. Miss L—— eyed me with disdain. "You're not trying to
get me quiffy?"

"No, I'm just—"

I dived for her body in haste—was this the moment? The
next half hour passed in close contact, small but firm rebuffs,
sweaty attacks, a few powerful slaps that caused my ear to sing.
However, as usual in our encounters, our healthy desires merged
to a point, so that I had my hands on her naked breasts under
her blouse and was kissing her mouth, nose, neck, throat in slob-
bering delight, and at last her nipples. We had kicked off our
shoes. It was a dozen dreams I'd had of this moment come true.
But as yet, no final penetration. Both of us were rumpled and
a little taut and moistly limber in the joints.

I nuzzled her fine tits with the top of my head, put my weight
on her chest and stomach, held on to her as-yet-clothed ass.
I felt primitive, but under control.

"I love you. There isn't anybody else in the world like you.
Slip off your drawers."

"You're a sweet boy, but you're too physical somehow, for
your age. No, *no!*"

She was aware of my state and of my weight on her—but
she was a powerfully muscled girl; goddamn all tennis courts and
Indian club drills at the Y.W.

"We're not like the rest of the damn town. We're artists in
a way."

"You will stop *when* I say so?"

I swore an oath better than Magna Charta.

She was fumbling at my fly and I aided her. She had my
dick out and in her fingers. I kissed her harder and put my hand
under her skirt and got the rubber band of her drawers in a
firm hand grip. I had expected the usual delaying resistance, which
took at least half an hour of pleading, sudden movements, rebuffs,

and promises of being good and restrained, to overcome the lowering of cotton. But now I had no trouble sliding the drawers down around her ankles, and with a pull I had them off. I kneaded the soft, yet at the same time, firm, belly; I rubbed her thighs. I pulled her toward me.

"I love your ass—I love my finger in your navel."

She rolled her head away from me, resisted my engineering efforts to spread her legs; she lifted her knees into my chest when I tried to stroke her pubic hair. But with rolling and sighing and protests and guarding of her ruby I was at her split.

The gas fixture was boiling over the night clatter of insects, the old house was settling with banging noises, and then I realized it was all my blood buzzing loudly in my ears. I moved her hand from my cock. This was not the plan. We had done this mutual but separate climaxing before. If I was to get in, it had to be before we both slacked off, before we triggered and Miss L—— was back to the restating of her virginity. I was astride her like a hard-riding western hero. She bucked me off with ease, for while I was strong, she was tennis-court hard, fast-at-the-net conditioned. I didn't want to use force in any brute action. I put teeth to nipples which keyed a frenzy of pain and pleasure. I wound arms about her hips, felt the pressure of all my focus in this one moment.

It was a matter of mere trajectory now, I figured, my head groggy, my mouth open, my groin and loins racked by ground glass. The strong straight line of Euclid—I must now risk all. My last reserves were committed.

A bit of voice, thick and gasping on my ear. "Grandpa—is he still rocking up in his room?"

"Yes."

A moment of complete passivity.

"Dear boy, *why* do you want more?"

I parted cunt lips of private warmth. I drove for the breach. Miss L—— twisted aside with strength. I fell onto the floor. My flesh had touched the forbidden zone for one fraction of a moment. There was the scent of two bodies in the gas-heated room; realities of our sweat, our moistures, the used and reused air. It was our remaining clothes, I decided, that hindered us. I had only my shirt and top of my underwear on. She only a skirt around her ankles. Petticoat and all else was gone. I grasped my grandfather's flask and took a deep suck; alcohol, I had heard, dulls passion, but I had enough to spare and I feared I'd splash over. My only worry was not to come too soon. I held out the flask and Miss L—— head down, eyes half closed, turned away. I pulled back her head and poured brandy into her mouth. She clenched her teeth. I did get a good portion of brandy down her throat. I got rid of my shirt; she resisted my removing the skirt after the stockings were gone.

"You've got to understand. Not *that*, dear boy."

"I know. I was carried away."

We were getting a second wind. She nuzzled my cheeks. I returned the pressure, feeling under the urge a weariness now, images of labia majora fading away. I heard the church clock in the Dutch Reformed strike the hour. I locked Miss L—— in my arms and with a great ache and a burning I applied all my pressure, all my weight, to keep her prone. I no longer heard the defense of virginity, of the hoarded gift to the phantom husband who would one day come into his own. I put the elbow of my arm against her neck. I wedged myself down between her limbs. I saw in the gaslight, the triangular curl of hair, the pink edges of her cunt... snarling (nearly), weeping too at the idea of victory, in one moment, I would penetrate Miss L—— and leave for the war with a first victory... no reticence, no shame, I jammed.

At that moment Miss L—— hit me over the head with a large brass Arab tray that rested on a low shelf over the sofa. I went black, came to with a lump behind my ear, a spinning room in my vision, a hell of a banging headache. Miss L——in her skirt and open shirtwaist, her tits like her face crimson with hurt disapproval, was bending over me... Florence Nightingale ministering to the wounded.

"I thought I had killed you."

"No," I said, shaking my head. "I've a hard skull." I was ashamed of my erection which had not yet understood the situation. I climbed into my B.V.D.s, hopping on one leg while I tried to put on my pants. When I had my shirttail tucked in place, I rolled my head back to get my damp hair out of my face. I was sad.

"I didn't want to hurt you; you must believe that."

"You're a cock-teaser Miss L——."

"That's a vulgar word. You're going away angry."

I hunted tie, coat, shoes, flask, left the tin of Trojans fallen silently onto the rug, six unborn orgasms. She moved toward me. I stepped back.

"No, you'd only hold out on me."

I felt what was the use? I had been banging for nearly two hours against a mirage; my stomach felt full of acid, my testicles heavy with dry cinders. I collected myself, my apparel, and any-which-way dressed. I went out into the hall, my bladder full. The lousy old man overhead was no longer rocking.

What a hell of a way to send a hero off to war. Writing about it now I can be ironic, and kidding the boy I was than. But it was bruising to my vanity and cut down my confidence for some time with women—at least for two weeks. I wrote Miss L—— letters of orgies all the next year. She was a lousy letter writer.

The Muslin Wings

Which Way to the War?

I was pretty ass-dragging low when I got back to Canada, after my defeat by Miss L——. But with more flying and two more deaths, more gunnery practice and some hell raising in town, I came out of my funk and looked forward to getting to the war zone and that war. I could just see Miss L—— reading the newspaper headline: LOCAL HERO DIES GALLANTLY IN AIR BATTLE, and she feeling, what price cunt now? The only part that didn't appeal to me was dying for that newspaper story. Was she worth it? Of course not.

Chunky was building model planes and figuring out how to scientifically attack the enemy in the air. John was avoiding the widow whose cooking and keep he liked. Something about being the father of an unborn child. But the field captain said, "Don't worry, she claimed that one last year and never dropped no kid. Anyway you leave tomorrow for jolly ol' England."

On an overpacked train one cold winter night near dawn, with a blizzard beating against Mr. Pullman's Palace Car windows, we lay in our berths hoping to beat the ice into the St. Lawrence. The telegraph poles went by on a slant, passing the express trains with their roar of red fire, rows of yellow windows, and the bong bong of our steel on good ballasted track. Here we were, John said, going far out "over the rounded surface of the globe heading to England, to war over the seas." I remembered my grandfather reading from Homer of "the wine-dark sea" and the "pink-fingered dawn" and was homesick—the way I had been going off to prep school.

The oddly painted Cunarder we boarded, pounding on at a steady series of knots, came with us seasick, tooting into Liverpool, the city all soot and dirt, gray and brown bricks. It was Saturday, and we three chums were a bit pale, standing there at the rail, damn lonely so far from home. The women in uniform were all long of tooth, the officers with pips on their uniforms all goddamn snotty. The dirty sweat-smelling boat train was smaller than any we had ever seen, and its whistle had a shrill, ladylike toot. The people, Chunky insisted, spoke a strange tongue that was nearly related to what we had been taught. "Lousy broad-ass *as*," said John. I had this feeling like I had crapped in my pants first day in kindergarten—but I tried to get excited by the rainy faded landscape—where the hell was the England of *The White Company*, Kipling, and Sherlock Holmes?

At the hollow glass-roofed London station the fog hung yellow in slowly moving coils, and the smell of coal burning and wet streets and cold pork sandwiches mixed with axle grease and the damp woolen clothes of the pale worried Londoners, didn't seem a proper welcome. No bands, no damn peach-skinned lady to kiss us.

Chunky said we stood "like survivors of an Indian raid," with our traveling bags, our mufflers tight around our throats as the cold came up through the stone floor and bit into our bodies.

A neat young officer with sickly classic features, dressed in an overcreased uniform with an RFC insignia, came over smiling. "You're the Canadians. Follow me."

"Americans," I corrected.

"You're all Americans over there. You mean USA."

Chunky said, "Well, kick my shaggy ass."

"The bloody war will, Yank. This way to a cabbie."

The taxi went slowly along in the pea-soup mist, and John wondered how people could live in this climate. We were pretty low.

"It isn't always this depressing, chaps. Sometimes it just rains. But we'll not stay here. You're to train in Camels—then on your way to France in a few weeks."

That nearly cheered us up.

"Never been out of the States before?" he asked.

I said, "Canada."

"Of course, Canada."

The cab rubbed against a great horse-drawn dray carrying barrels of Royal Crest Stout and Ale.

"Some Americans over here giving you blokes a dinner."

The dinner was dull. We saw our first live English butler. Our hostess, in a low-cut velvet gown, kept swinging her long string of pearls from a plump hand. "Oh, dear, this war—it's unthinkable. Utterly."

I dreamed crazy that night in my too-narrow hotel room of the scarlet lobster alive in its mayonnaise dressing crawling over my pillow, then down to nip at my pecker. I slept till the boy called Boots came to knock on the door with the morning paper—GREAT BATTLE ON SOMME. We three Yanks gingerly ate kidneys grilled, and found the coffee as dreadful as the weather. We moved out and the next few weeks we flew Camels in Essex, saw more young fliers die, learned how to use the

Lewis gun, the Vickers gun, read maps, remember signals, keep our bowels open, drink 'arf and 'arf, fuck standing up against a stone wall. We were so damn earnest and eager to get to France, the gunnery sarge had to keep saying: "Better learn to 'andle yer guns me young sods, first."

I was learning life was damn precious—and I was betting against the game of God's dice, with the odds way against me. The fliers were dying at a fearful rate in France. It was no good to tell myself, "Nobody dies at seventeen." Seventeen was death's favorite age in the air.

Chunky got a rusty nail into his foot through his boot, and went to hospital, and there was in hope of getting a beautiful nurse (he mentioned Mrs. Pat Campbell, Lilly Langtry, Ellen Terry). He'd been reading English magazines. But he told us when we brought him hot-house grapes in sawdust, his nurse was a horror. "Smells like rotting clams, but has a marvelous moustache." John was in a darts contest weekends at the bar of the Royal Crown. So I went one weekend to Canterbury. I don't know why. Two weekends in London had been only fair. The city busy with the war, but getting shabby, and the tarts in a hurry. "All them chaps on leave, from 'olding it back in them trenches." When I paid one whore with a gold coin, she put it in her mouth for safe keeping while we did a quick five minutes of panting.

I was impressed by the cathedral in Canterbury, and the size of it, and how old it looked, and I felt a bit disgusted with my hedonism—I had found the word in a book...I liked the look of old stone and wormy wood. Bulk and surfaces that look as if they've had a hard life. Well, that was my mood all through the training in England. I never got to like the warm beer, tripe and onions, or the way the quality at parties said, "Oh, Americans."

I liked the English girls we met at teas and dances; no tits most of them, but long-legged, pink-cheeked, marvelous nostrils, and you wouldn't believe their underwear. Knickers they call their drawers, and they'd pour tea and milk at the same time into the cup like it was natural—maybe it was.

Then we were leaning uncertainly on the rail of a blacked-out channel steamer, the smoke of the funnel being torn to shreds by a brisk wind from France ("Fair stood the wind for..."). Officers were holding their belted stomachs as the steamer dipped and tossed, till someone said *that* thin bloody line was bloody Calais.

"Calais?" Chunky asked, pointing. "Looks like Asbury Park."

"Oh, yes, that's hit," said a Cockney batman. "Bloody fukking plice hit is, too. The hures all over fifty and no teef."

The French landscape from the train looked a great deal like being home, only the houses were older and all of solid stone—until we saw some ruins. The first look at Paris came on us with the chatter of what could only be French, and we rode in pale daylight in an open car marked B.E.F. among the bare chestnut trees, and saw the spires of Notre Dame overhead. John, who read art magazines, said, "Isn't at all like the Pissaros and the Manets."

We stayed at the Hotel Meurice on the Rue de Rivoli, and we couldn't even unpack. Chunky asked what was that strange little floor spray in the bathroom. A twat flush, we found out. It got to be a *very* tired joke.

"Too short a day to waste by just resting," I said. John said, "We move to Arras tonight. Let's see the Tuileries Gardens and walk to the Place de la Concorde."

"What about Les Girls?" asked Chunky.

It was a city all very shabby and war-tired. Wide unswept boulevards, ill-dressed people, a smoky sky, the few bits of pale green making it a sad picture all the length of the Champs-Elysees. One girl clung to John's arm. She smelled of candied violets and sour wine.

"Uloo, Tommy, Zig-zig wif me?"

"After the war."

"Go 'ump your grandmere."

That afternoon John was examined by an RFC flight doctor who said John's sense of balance was wrong; we were to leave for Arras without him. He saw us to the train station. There we found the wounded being carried away and lots of dirty drunk French infantry, big moustaches, tin hats, going back to the front from leave, women in dull black weeping, the station smelling of steam, piss, dried butchershop blood. Only it wasn't beef—it was the wounded. Oh, how gangrene stinks.

We had a last drink at a zinc and Chunky gave us a school song on his guitar.

> Wild roved an Indian girl, bright Alfarata
> Where sweeps the waters of the blue Juniata.

We sang in unison:

> I took my girl to a fancy ball,
> It was a social hop
> Then to the restaurant we went,
> The best one on the street.
> She said she wasn't hungry.
> And this is what she'd eat...

Chunky took up the refrain:

> A dozen raw, a plate of slaw,
> A chicken and a roast,
> Some sparrow grass with apple sass,
> And soft shell crabs on toast.
> A big box stew with crackers too,
> Her hunger was immense.
> When she called for pie, I thought I'd die,
> For all I had was fifty cents.

Then Chunky and I ran to make our train, and I was sure I would be dead in four to six weeks... if lucky. The unlucky fliers lasted a week or two. Everybody we met was happy to tell us of the short life of fliers at the front.

I remember a latrine sign: FOR WHAT KING, WHAT COUNTRY? I have only a kind of torn film as memory of the first two months in France at a British air base. It is like when the film runs fast and tears and shakes, and you catch on screen an eye staring and an arm gesturing. But it doesn't make too much sense. Maybe I was scared shitless (actually it was the other way around—I got constipated—solid cement). Maybe I was still a kid acting bushy-tailed and snotty. The British fliers weren't much older, but some survivors had fingers that trembled and cut themselves shaving. Some stood at the officers' bar a lot, glass in hand—just nodding or saying, "Oh, hard cheese," or "Who? No, gone west."

I did a week of solos, some gunnery practice. Then I was part of a patrol that was in very safe territory indeed. Chunky had some Heinie bullet holes in a wing and one week later got a German. Christ, to celebrate, we got loaded and sick, catted up last week's meals. Three days later, I saw two of ours shot down, go smoking and twisting down, down and I yelled, "No! No!" I hedgehopped back to base and found I had pissed my boots full... Impressions... torn images. Nothing to relate in any order.

Two days later, I somehow fired my guns at a wing with a Maltese cross on its varnished muslin and I got my first kill. That's what it was like for an American flying with the RFC in France early in the war.

That winter we were flying over the front from the Wing Headquarters aerodrome behind Amiens. It was a bloody, blue-cold winter; the squadron was using Sopwith Camels, nearly as bad as DH4s, the goddamn notorious Flaming Coffins. We pilots lived on milk and brandy, stinking of tension turned to sweat in our black flying breeks, going over the Hun lines, escorting the heavy reconnaissance camera planes with the enemy's Archies exploding high up, bursting in our faces. The legend that nobody lived beyond the first six weeks was mostly true. In the British Sixth Wing, actually by count, we lost a third of our flyers, and it got worse before Cambrai fell, when the Boche began mounting heavier Spandau machine guns in their gaddamn Jagdstaffel—hunting packs. They had replaced their older planes with the Fokker triplane, and we were still in the flypaper and canvas and wood Sopwith F.1 Camels. With us, Chunky said, it was the will doing the work of the impossible. We all took to carrying bottles of brandy in our coverall leg pockets.

Flying on patrol, the long-toothed major with the trick pipe got his, trying out a new Nieuport over the lines (as expected the air valve jammed and the engine conked). He tried to climb vertically, went into a slow roll and a loop. A Hun dipped down out of the sun and began to pour it into him, and I saw the major's face, the Sandhurst moustache standing out. I was flying on his left tip, trying to come up to protect him. He just looked disappointed, mouthed the word *merde*, and the crate began to smoke and flame and slide down, discarding wings and parts. He waved, I thought—these buggering British—the willed gesture that becomes a principle. (I was reading books with footnotes between missions. The horseshit of philosophy.)

I didn't follow the major down because I was trying to get the sun between me and the red-streaked Fokker, and when I had him in the sights, I prayed that the rotten mechanical device that synchronized my two Lewis guns to fire through the propeller would work. A week before I had shot off my own prop and landed in the middle of an Anzac battalion in the lines. I had been sweating it out, for the wind was always blowing to the east and there was the danger of coming down behind the German lines.

I fired a burst to clear the barrels and the blur of the spinning prop was all right. Oh, the Hun was good. He tried to keep the sun behind me, but the petrol in my tanks was clean that morning, and I circled and got him on his tail, he twisting, me after him, the Teutonic crosses on his wings black against the dark canvas. I pressed off half a drum right into him and the sonofabitch didn't seem to hurt at all. I could see wood and canvas splintering off and falling away. We had become a deadly tight duet, stuck close, to the death.

He lifted away to climb and I throttled back and thought fuckyoukraut, when I sensed something on my right, and there I was jumped by a staffel of Albatrosses who were laying for me. My pigeon had been a decoy. I kicked the stick over and went into a long, fast dive, wires screaming, did an evasion spin that began to strain the wings, and I cursed the profiteers who cheated on aeroplane specifications. There was a wisp of cloud nearby, looking no bigger than a bath towel, and I started for that and it was bigger than it looked. I was very young and didn't want to die. Not before I sent my grandmother a picture of myself in my London-tailored uniform and my grandfather some French postal cards.

I went through the cloud and found myself with just one Hun. He had a skull and bones painted on his canvas side, and I automatically pressed the Lewis button and a staccato burst caught him in the belly of his machine. I was just under him—in his blind spot—and he fell, all black smoke, flames redder than any paint job. I could see the flier's protuberant bloodshot eyes as he screamed. Nobody carried parachutes in those days, and his right wing just touched mine—a kiss—as he fell away in a big gray world.

I scooted for our lines, sticky with fear. I vomited brandy and milk and bile all over my instrument panel. Yes, it was very romantic flying, people said later, like a knight errant in the clean blue sky of personal combat, in whipcord breeches and a British tunic with long Bond-Street-cut tails. So romantic...oh shit and piss. I remembered an old Sunday school lesson: "Man is full of misery and all earthly beauty is corrupt because of the untiring abjuration of the Devil..."

I was sobbing and my mouth, throat, sour-tasting like acid when I came over our dusty aerodrome and set the plane down with a hard bounce—a bad show of nerves The ack emma warrant officer came out in the windy cold among the trampled weeds, the Lewis gunnery sergeant at his side.

"The major bought one," I said, climbing out, covered with my own slime.

"We heard. One of the Handley Page chaps saw it."

"Major was due for leave, too," said the gunnery sergeant, examining my guns. "You 'ad 'ardly anything left in the Lewis drums."

I wanted to smoke. I didn't want to smoke. I walked toward the tin hut where the flight officer would want to hear it officially. It was too warm in the hut, a small stove ate coke, gave off gas, and used up the air. Captain H——, M.C., D.S.M., sat at a desk, a gray scarf wound around his neck, his Savile Row boots scuffed. He looked like a proper advertisement for the paraphernalia of war, only his eyes were bloodshot, and he had a small tic on his right cheek.

"Phone call just came in. Your kill confirmed. Your third?"

I poured myself a brandy from the desk bottle, knocked it back..."I want to go to Arras on leave. I've shot my load."

"Arras? All right."

"I'll take a bath."

"Saved you a steak. We killed a Frenchie's cow, by accident. Envy you the cossie in Arras." He made an obscene thumb-jabbing gesture. I went to the bathhouse and fell asleep standing under the hot shower and nearly scalded myself. I left the flying jacket and the gear for the batman to take to the laundress. I must have slept open-mouthed for some time because when I woke up the sun was on the dirty windowpane and my mouth was the Black Hole of Calcutta. The colonel with the ADM had his gramophone going: "There's A Long Long Trail A-Winding."

The field major of our unit—we called him "Old Maj"—was elderly for a flier, even a grounded one. He must have been thirty-eight at least. He had fought the Boers as a horse soldier in South Africa, "the filthiest humans on earth, just like their Hun cousins," and had flown with A. V. Roe, who later made the Avro fighter plane. He told us after a few whiskeys how the four squadrons sent to France at the outset of war turned out to be thirty-seven planes actually ready on English fields, with twenty-six more set to join them in a couple of days, maybe. Painted a dull olive and numbered in squadrons from 2 to 5. The first British machine to join the war in France went to a B.E.2A, No. 2 Squadron. The pilot was Lt. H. D. Harvey-Kelly, "my chum," said Old Maj. Just before 6:30 in the morning of August 13, 1914, Harvey-Kelly's plane took the air outside Dover, to come down at Amiens two hours later, less five minutes. The rest of the squadrons followed, some that day and some two days later. "We were flying a motley collection of planes: B.E.2s, Morane-Saulnier Parasols, Blériots, B.E.8s, Avro 504s and Farmans. Secondary and third-stage versions of the Wright brothers' ideas of flying. Engines none too reliable, frames of wood with stretched muslin wings, varnished, struts and wires hardly strong enough to take the strain of pressure or diving speed." The fixed wheels did not look tough enough to withstand the jolt of landings in the pastures that passed for airfields. The machines stank of petrol and shook like nervous dogs; yet they flew.

Old Maj dug up a list I still have. Every British flier had this official list of what he was to carry: extra flying goggles, some sort of tool kit, field glasses, boiled water in a canteen, a kind of cooking stove, biscuits, cans of corn beef, chocolate bars. Weapons: a revolver and cartridges. "Fucking Alice-in-Wonderland White-Knight scene, what?"

Sent over the channel by boat were four City of London vans provided to transport luggage and gear that could not be carried by plane. "No time to paint out their London lettering—Bovril Beef Cubes, Lazenby's Sauce, Stephen's Blue Black Ink, Peak Frean's Biscuits, and some music hall posters. End of 1914, we had sixty-three or sixty-four planes over here by the meadows and oh, a hundred or a hundred and five fliers, good chaps. All gone, most of them...oh, well...Who's holding back the damn whiskey?"

Flying the War

After I got my bearings I began to sort things out. The first aerodromes, flying fields, were just huts, tents and hangars resting on mud. The shoddy construction of everything that housed men and planes was the best of the usual official fuckup. Cubbyhole rooms, sleeping quarters cluttered with maps, binoculars, dogs, a few cats, even several monkeys shivering with cold. Everywhere smelly clothes, busted-up mementos of the war, shattered propellers, patches of enemy wing insignia cut from downed planes, parts of burned-out motors used as paperweights. Like a rundown prep school dorm. On walls group photographs of fliers, a goodly percentage rotting now—their ghost arms around survivors, ugly pictures of dead enemy fliers, or friends mutilated by exploding dumdums. Broken kids in charred twisted death... A scattering of magazines, pipes, tobacco jars, yellow-bound novels, little boxes of stomach pills.

Chunky was doing better than I was, plump, short, apple-faced Chunky. I was no hero, but I did many brave things. Because one did things one didn't do at home, or react normally. It was soon clear in your view of the war that you didn't give a shit for England, France, the Allies, or for glory or fame. You were brave because your aerodrome, your group, was your whole world. The cheerful or gloomy pricks you drank with, sang with, went hunting food, wine, women on leave with, were all you had. You drove crazy cars with them—cried and comforted each other through the shakes; you just could not act brave. It was pride, it was ego. In the end it was loyalty to those you saw and flew with that put the solid cement in your backbone. It was the same way, you saw, with the Frenchies. The Escadrille Les Coqs and Les Cigognes. There was some place an Escadrille Américaine, that became the Escadrille Lafayette when the Heinies objected to a neutral country having its name on an enemy fliers groupe de chasse.

The space we lived in—bar, reading room, mess, concert hall—Chunky called "our home away from home." Space was given to religious tracts, texts on national pride, glory, the nobility of the causes fliers were dying for; and newspapers printed specifically for the armed forces. Music was obtainable on a stolen piano, but mostly the old hand-wound gramophone and its scratchy, whining records was music. "Coon songs," ragtime favorites, vaudeville entertainers, Irving Berlin, George M. Cohan, Chauncey Olcott, Al Jolson. The English preferred music-hall entertainers. A favorite was Harry Tate, a comic of slow and hilarious delivery. The fliers named the RE-8 reconnaissance biplane, one of the worst planes of the war, the "Arry Tate."

Our airfield and buildings were overrun by dogs—barking, mating, birthing litters. There were cats for ratting and mousing, pet monkeys, often a goat. A stern commander of an aer-

odrome could keep some kind of order and a surface
cleanliness. Much in the bad or nonregulation conduct of fliers
was deliberately overlooked. Lives as active fliers were short,
and there seemed little sense in bringing us before a military
court when we might be dead or prisoner before it sat. Deco-
rated national heroes were hardly likely to be tried for being
drunk, abusing a superior officer, attempting rape, or comman-
deering an official car or truck.

Booze was the big problem. Legally or through connec-
tions, brandy, whiskey, and cognac were available. Pilots went
to bed drunk and usually returned from leaves in a very shaky
condition. Battle fatigue, war nerves, light mental breakdowns
were treated as "the shakes," "jollies," "the wind up," or just
plain "bugs," unless violent or dangerous to limb or property.
The medical staff did little beyond body patching and advice
to "slack off a bit."

Gambling was another outlet from the tension of being on
patrol duty, flying over the front. Americans in the RFC introduced poker and crap shooting. But for those who had been
raised on whist and bridge, roulette at Monte, the royal flush
or the rattling dice seemed vulgar. Reading was an escape from
immediate reality. Arnold Bennett, Galsworthy, Conan Doyle,
Edgar Wallace, Edgar Rice Burroughs, Zane Grey were often
found in a dead airman's luggage when a batman packed it for
his next of kin.

And always the gramophone going: "There's a Long Long
Trail A-Winding..." I had come out of sleep as if from a cave.
My throat was raw. All dimensions and echoes had lost their
outer reality for me. A sure sign a flier is nerve-taut, is living
off gut power alone.

I got up and took a pick-me-up brandy, and I wished I had
a couple of raw eggs to go with it, the way my grandfather used
to drink and wink. "Man is the creature of obligations and betray-
als, but a good toot of whisky never did a soul harm."

There was a tap on the door and I mumbled something…A tall man came in—one of the most handsome dark rabbinical men I've ever seen. This must be the Jewboy replacement.

"Hello Lieutenant, I'm Tony P——."

We shook hands. He had that soft curly hair and those big dark eyes, very big ones, violet pupils that women fall right into bed for when they see them. There was a tight caul on my skull and I didn't feel I had any charm to spare.

"Have a drink. How many hours you solo." He looked very smart, puttees, ordnance belt, all the brass and expensive leather of a fresh replacement. He held out a tin of Papastratos cigarettes, a gold lighter.

"Enough, enough. This looks like a crackerjack outfit."

"We've what's left of other squadrons. The remains are put in here." We smoked slowly. "Tony, the planes are not too good, but the mechanics are wonders and the C.O. a decent sort of prick, doesn't care what you do so long as you salute and go up when your squadron leader says, 'Let's go, chaps.'"

"What have you been flying?" I asked.

"The Martinsyde, some Nieuports."

"What guns you train with?"

"Vickers."

"We use Lewis—usual air force balls-up."

My batman Hughie came in with a tray. He wore the Mons Star and some lower award that was given to the rank and file. He lifted the tin lid off some poached eggs. "Stole these Leftenant, and the coffee is the real thing. Too bad about the major. One of the best, as they say."

"The very best. This is Lieutenant P——. Get him a batman who knows the gear. Tony, Hughie Green—a marvelous thief. Steal the scales off a snake."

"Right as rain, sir," said Hughie.

He went out and I stared at the eggs and swallowed the very black coffee with the four spoons of sugar in it.

"What's there in Arras?"

"Tail, booze."

He looked at a fragment of a Boche wing with a cross on it, a splintered prop off an Albatross D-III that killed our last squadron leader. "I'm a Jew, you know."

"Wouldn't have guessed," I said.

"Don't want anybody saying the goddamn Heeb, he's got yellow crap up his back."

"Look, Tony. The trick is, figure the odds. One-third of the fliers go west on a front like this in two weeks, two-thirds of the fliers survive a month. Half of them crap out—mental. It's very quiet just now. Too cold."

Outside they were starting up the afternoon patrol. I could smell the burning castor oil they were mixing with the lubrication, hear the young carnivores in flying suits chattering—most of them celibate, pink-cheeked, earnest. I handed Tony the plate of poached eggs.

"Eat this. In a couple of weeks you may not like solid food." I went out to see about transportation to Arras. The patrol was in the air, trying to get over the trees.

A fighter pilot's view of life on the ground is narrow, and sits on rumors. The lie was the Germans in the air or on the ground weren't as good as we were, weren't fighting up to snuff any more. Of course the generals sitting snug on their prostates in their big Rolls-Royces with an aide carefully putting the woolen rug over their legs and paunches, insisted in interviews: *Sacrifice was Glory.* It was *for Civilization, for Mankind.* We fliers were pretty sick of abstractions. Vaterland, Freedom, Democracy, The King. The Prince of Wales (poor creepy young bastard in his tight little uniform, his sleepy eyes half open, moving down a safe trench and shaking hands with little undernourished Cockneys). It was a war for no reason. We didn't see much hope of surviving. It was all a bloody sellout, and we fliers now were aware of it. "All our own fault," Chunky said.

I was trying to think. It hurt. As I flew I wasn't buying
Father O'Bein, or Church of England's Cecil, or Rabbi Hauk-
fliesh and all their fine moral promises and splendid dogmas.
Because there were O'Beins and Cecils and Haukflieshs on the
other side too. God in that war was divided from his crotch to
his eyebrows. He promised victory through O'Bein, etc., to
those who had the faith. I didn't have faith, only a hatred of
official cant. I was becoming an alcoholic, I had crabs, two cavities in my back teeth. I couldn't at times control the twitch on
my face. My hands had a tremor. I had murdered half a dozen
Germans or Austrians or Rumanians who were out to murder
me. And almost everything I and John and Chunky had
believed in as boys was merde—plain shit, smelly, oh *so* smelly.
Fortunately for me I went raving, flaming mad when it got too
much. But that came later. I always thought I faked it beauti-
fully, the grimaces, the twitching, the filthy language. But doctors told me, "No, old boy, you had really gone off your rocker."

I got a good leave. I had on a clean uniform, my best
unpaid tailored one. The poor London bugger waited years for
payment. I had my swagger stick. ("Phallic?" Chunky once
asked. "Like the English prick in hand, public exhibitionists?")
I had a nice alcohol glow, I was shaved, cap over one eye; was
standing in the flight officer's hut, waiting for the grease mon-
key to change a tire on the officers' mess car, a beat-up Bentley.
Free for two days from the laws of inevitability. And in Arras.
Not Paris. Not London. But a city.

A muddy Renault came up the wreck of a muddy road
from the main highway, and under the camouflage nets. Four
officers in RAF dress were singing "The Bastard King of England." They were all very young, very Anglo-Saxon; you could
almost use them as a poster. One waved. It was John B——.

I hadn't seen John since 1916 when we had come over on
a boat from Canada and he had flunked the coordination tests
(they claimed his sense of balance had been damaged as a boy

in some sport accident). He looked very solid. There were flying
wings on his tunic and French and English chicken-shit of gold
and silver and bronze.

Chunky was by his side, opening the twisted wires on the
cork of a wine bottle. The two officers in the back I didn't
know. Chunky got out and slapped me on the back. "See who
I found?" John got out and slapped me on the back, and I met
the two other officers. They didn't slap me on the back. Oxford
kids, pink-cheeked, foul-mouthed in a cute way, very friendly,
but numb as if anesthetized at some rites.

John smiled, showing the even row of good teeth and the
capped one he had shattered. "Imagine you still alive. We were
running low on petrol and I met Chunky; said let's run in here
and steal some."

"I'll get the gunnery sergeant; that's his swindle. Where you
stationed?"

"With the Air Group some place near Ypres. It's a bitched-
up war, isn't it?"

Chunky said, as the cork came out, "They took him when
they'd killed off all the young folk with good balance." He
sucked up champagne and put his arms around me and hugged
me. "You don't see any of our strong stern breed out here. But
soon, eh, soon? The whole American Army."

One of the Oxford boys nodded. "You'll win the whole
bloody hairy-arsed war for us, you Yanks."

"That we will. Want to fight?" asked John. He needed a
haircut, his nose had been broken, he was too lean. "Never
stick it into an ally, old chap."

"Where you all going?" I asked. I wanted to tell John how
pleased I was to see him, but it made me sad to admit I missed
anybody.

"Some estaminet, the Cloche-Clos, Kevin has an old uncle
there in the Engineers. We want to borrow a few hundred
nickers. Maybe go to Paris."

A Paris Wedding

Only we didn't get to Paris that time. The big push to try and capture Cambrai came and all squadrons went up to take on the Jagdstaffels. Both of the English boys were killed first time up. When Chunky placed their things he found one boy had marked a book:

> By my troth, I care not; a man can die but once,
>   we owe God a death...and let it go which way it will,
>   he that dies this year, is quit for the next...

Of course it was fancy literary horseshit. Shakespeare was whistling passing a graveyard.

Later the weather had been a gray bowl of sky, so bad we couldn't fly any sorties over the front at our sector based beyond Arras. The war lay under a lashing rain, and the morning mists lasted all day, and below us men drowned in mud, so stinking it was part man, mule, and horse—all dead. Chunky, from his squadron, drove up to the aerodrome one morning gay as a grig, in a 12.5 horsepower Sizaire that had one big headlight over its radiator like Cyclops' eye. Chunky, in a long clipped sheepskin coat, pink whipcord breeches, splendid Savile Row boots, looked the tight-assed proper ace. He had the M.C. and I was now a captain and had the D.S.M., and solid gold insignia on my cap. Oh, we were the fancy stuff to feed the folks back home in newspaper stories and interviews and photos. If you didn't notice the twitch in our cheeks and the stylish tremor in the nicotined fingers. The French called us l'as de notre aviation acés.

"Paris, for our major's wedding," he said.

"Same girl?"

"Of course, the same girl."

I noticed a huge shaggy dog on the front seat of the auto. "What the hell is that?"

"Wedding gift for the major. Genuine Boche dog, survived a crash when our group shot down a Heinie ace, his master, in his Albatross. You'd have loved it. I'm flying at three thousand feet, see, and out of a cloud comes this cocksucker above me, sun in my eyes, I nearly shat but took a fast wing roll to the left and..."

"I've got to wangle leave from the CO. Three days enough?"

"More than. Bring any buddy you have. Très gash, très likker, comprendez-vous?"

The group major was sitting at his desk under the signed photograph of Guynemer and his Spad, and a small model of the DH4 in which the major lost his left foot flying over Ypres in the early days. His overbred face—like a racehorse—tired.

"We want to bomb Bissege aerodrome soon as this muck clears. HQ is chewing out my arse why we're not flying right now...Paris? Out of the question. Fearfully sorry."

"Must be at the wedding. Both of us likely to crap out on any flight. Odds against us ever meeting again."

The major did a slow assimilation of my words. "Have the warrant officer give you the pass. And pray there's no sunshine for three days."

"I'd like to take Tony P——. He's the only survivor of his replacement group."

"Been lucky, hasn't he? Oh, and steal me a bottle of Hennessy Three Star, like a good chap."

Tony wasn't half pleased to be getting away to Paris. He had turned out to be a marvelous flier, but I couldn't see how he'd live much longer. He had a habit of drifting east across the lines at two thousand feet, and waiting till a group of von Kleinschmidt's Fokker triplanes came out at noon, regular as clockwork. Then Tony would dive in among them, his wings almost tearing out, and pick off one or two before they knew he was there. They'd go into attack and evasion movements thinking it was an RAF group squadron attack. By that time, Tony was either flying low for home over the lines, or cutting off a Hun who had made the wrong move and was alone and vulnerable to the twin Lewis guns pumping tracers into the enemy canvas and wood and living meat. But they were getting wise to Tony and dividing up; some day soon they'd bracket Tony and his damn Camel between them. The Spandau slugs would give us another dead ace. We had plenty of those. The major considered Tony a very soigné type and related to the Rothschilds. He wasn't.

"The bride pretty?" asked Tony, admiring his dark good looks in a mirror as he buttoned on his London cut jacket.

"Not as pretty as you are. Never met her."

Outside, Chunky was honking the horn of the car. I had left him in the mess bar drinking doctored Scotch on my slate.

The canvas top of the Sizaire was only fairly waterproof, but we had our trench coats on, and between the bottle of brandy and some singing, and the dog Fritz barking, we managed to get stuck only twice in the foul mud the roads had become under four years of horse manure, army traffic, and shelling. It was sad to see the long lines of boys and middle-aged men marching the other way, wet, muddy, burdened with firearms and war gear. The French were scraping up old men now, ancient farts with whiskers and rounded bony shoulders. The English were mostly mere runty kids, whey-faced, lips blue with rain. The horse-drawn wagons were miserable, everything worn and unpainted till you came across some American equipment which looked show-off strange and like a too-new toy until the mud covered it.

Chunky bent over the steering wheel of the iron monster. "We Yanks, we'll have to end it for them."

Tony beat his swagger stick on his legs. "Paris. The Louvre. Notre Dame. I wonder if they still have the old bookstalls on the Seine."

Chunky took a suck of the brandy bottle and worked the hand-turned windshield wiper. "Bien mercie, et vous-même! Jew-boy, you out of your rabbinical mind? We're going to Paris to paint it red, marry off our Major, drink, eat, sleep and get laid. Eh, Fritz, du Schweinhund? Want your ashes hauled?"

The dog barked and clawed at Chunky from the back seat. Chunky steered the car around a horse-drawn 75 mired to the wheels. The flogged horses had given up; the Frenchmen, bearded muddy lumps, cursed us out, but with no strength or feeling in it.

"I could open this baby, open to a hundred miles an hour. The power of Niagara under the hood."

Tony said, "Let's try."

"It's a racer with the rear seat built on. After the war I'm going to take it down to Nice and open it up in a road race. After the war."

Tony took the nearly empty bottle. "Nobody, Chunky, unless it's the dog, is going to be around after the war."

Chunky grinned. "All I'm praying for is a nice clean wound,

just a flesh wound, see—and a nurse with beautiful tits and some English garden to convalesce in. I'm a Catholic. I believe in prayer. I'll include you guys in when I pray in Paris. What you rather have, a leg wound or an arm wound? Nothing irrational or bizarre. Just a wound."

Tony threw the empty bottle out into the rain beyond the flapping curtains. "Gunnery-Sergeant Peterson got his balls shot off. I'd rather get it between the eyes."

We hit a rut and the car bounced so high we came down on the shoulder of the road. Chunky sang: "Viens poupoule" and Tony offered "La Petite Tonkinoise." The dog and I didn't have any voice.

A Senegalese company of black colonials, blue-green with cold and damp, were huddled over smoldering little fires. They jumped apart as we passed splashing—scattered rifles, knives, miserable little pots of condemned canned stew they were heating, which the regulars wouldn't eat.

Chunky threw some franc notes at them as he plowed back onto the road. "Poor niggers, what are they fighting for?"

Tony said, "The right to eat their grandmothers. What are we fighting for?"

"To get passes to Paris," I said.

Chunky took his hand off the wheel and beat his gloved fists together. I grabbed the wheel as we passed a mired tank, its crew sitting under a canvas spread like shipwrecked sailors.

"Who the hell has a pass? I just went out over the gate our dustbins use."

Tony said cheerfully, "They'll shoot you. Six ack emma in the morning. Twelve rifles, one cigarette, one blindfold, one priest. Officer's coup de grâce behind the ear."

"They can't. I'm the only surviving member of the bloody squadron who can get the young squabs up in the air. Oh, it's shameful what we do—the poor little pissers, so game and so scared, rosy-cheeked. They belong on the playing fields of Eton or blowing upperclassmen, not going up against Staffel in our old AKWs. Here's a place to piddle and get that brandy."

We slid into a courtyard all manure pile under a grape arbor, leafless and black. Fritz snarled. Several lorries were in the yard lettered USA. The inn was full of deserters and apaches, maquereaux, momes hiding out from the army lists. "Je prends mon bien où je le trouve."

It wasn't raining so hard when we started up again.

Paris in wartime was a sad place, like a kick in the ass that didn't hurt. There was little paint, bits of missing glass were replaced by boards and cardboard. The streets were filthy, shutters hung on a slant. The staff cars—Rolls, Pierce-Arrows, Fiats, and fancy French jobs, all in battle gray or mustard, moved healthy looking officers around. Lorries seemed to be passing in neverending rows. Now and then a Ford ambulance rattled by us, and I didn't like the stains around the doors in back. Lots of legless and armless and blind men were around.

We had faked some kind of paper for Chunky on an old military form for Handley Page motor parts. I knew it wouldn't fool any English patrol. We detoured around the main gates into Paris and came up past the Gare de Lyon, crowded with returning leave trains, human cargoes going out to die or drown beyond the Marne. We went past hotels looking sodden in the thin green rain. I hoped I'd cheer up. After all the USA was in the war now.

The major, a rich boy from St. Louis, had taken a suite at the Ritz for the wedding. There was still a doorman, one empty sleeve pinned across his chest over his medals. We took Fritz in with us and the clerk said we weren't going to be allowed to have the creature along.

Tony said, "This is President Wilson's dog."

The clerk said it was by appearance, Monsieur, a Boche dog.

We went for the lift without waiting to hear any more.

The lobby was full of well-dressed, fine-smelling, meaty women, a few charming in lacy mourning black. There were assorted officers of all nations with that fine smooth look of desk riders, a Jesuit, a man who said he ran the prison of the Santé, staff pips, red-braided caps, fliers. There was a middle-aged French officer, one-legged and on crutches, talking to an Italian major with plucked eyebrows. And there was steam heat, something most hotels were leaving out that season. Ecstasy and excitement seemed on tap. Tony quoted Donne as he sniffed: "And what wind serves to advance an honest mind."

We knew the floor of the major's suite before we got there. A humming buzzing noise, a breakage of glass, a singing of some sentimental flying force ballad about taking the engine out of my liver, lift the crankcase from my chest.

Chunky's eyes gleamed. "Hear all that girl-laughter?"

War or not—money was money, and the red-carpeted hallway was heavy with waiters and maids pushing little tables of drink and food. The gold and white doors of the suite were open, and there a pattern of officers, and well-dressed women mixed together in tobacco smoke, retaining their hold on glasses of wine and hard stuff. The women were, I figured—rapidly taking inventory of haunches, arms, torsos, legs—one-third in uniform of some special HQ service, Red Cross, Admiralty, War Office; the helpers of wearying desk officers that relished the need of pretty girls to keep them alert in the office, warm. Comfortable in bed, and available for dinner or a long distasteful journey to some Legation or HQ. They, too, fought a splendid war. Basically, in war only three things matter (historians lie about it)—sexual congress, drunken plenty, and avoidance of death. The rest is merde.

Some of the women were in black, and the few men in frock coats had a sprinkling of mourning bands among them. They had survived their sons and, I figured, felt pious about it. One learned in three years of war to take death with the proper period of mourning—a dead hero never becomes a problem child. The black public sign of: *we, too, have had our loss, and so chin up. Drink in hand, carry on, the worst is yet to be.* There were Amer-

ican officers looking very Zeta Psi and Skull and Bones from
Yale. Couple of Harvard poets driving ambulances (I remember
Dos Passos being there).

Chunky went barging into other rooms. Tony and I grabbed
a waiter, cornered him, and before his pleased eyes had three
large champagnes each. "It's good," Tony said, "to know the French
had lots of vintage wine left."

We went to the buffet, smiled at the suckling pig, at the pink
sliced ham, at the spiced animal organs, sea life, tidbits in aspic,
caviar on ice, the smoked goose, the pâté with bay leaves. Tony
and I, so long alive on bad coffee, brandy, leathery eggs, canned
offal from the Chicago packing houses, smiled at each other and
fell to, mouths greasy, stomachs at rest now that we didn't have
to fly a dawn patrol. We looked about us. Chewing, sipping, eyes
on stems at the sight of the clean women. A small band played
Victor Herbert waltzes under some palms yellowing in gilt pots.
We took it all in with the unanesthetized parts of our brains.

Said Tony with awe, respect, "You ever see so much woman
even in your best dreams. God never made anything else as beautiful as a woman's buttocks."

I lead him over to the seafood buffet. "Stop pawing the ground
like a stud stallion."

It was a grand wedding and low life afterward. Three days
later—still hung over—I was flying escort to bomb a railroad
supply depot.

By late 1917 we tired rummies and crocks were aware of
how crazy and sick a war it was. After all the flying, the Vickers
gun bursts; no flags waving, no gallant charges, no Red Cross
nookie; maybe a hairy kiss on the cheeks by a French general.

As we flew we knew below us five, six million filthy men
were buried alive underground, living like crazy, red-eyed rats
in their own shit and piss, decaying comrades' entrails. Years of
burrowing, rotting away, dying with silly shocked gestures to gain,
retain, fifty yards, a hundred yards. Then back into the crap and

the cootie hells, the stink of unburied dead from 1914 on—all those rotting horses too. In the air we missed a war that smelled of manure, putrefying generations of dead schoolboys and fathers. We fliers could only smell it sometimes as we came in at dusk, back from patrol, flying low over the trenches that stretched in the earth from the English Channel to the Swiss. When you went to mess with the line officers, they smelled of it, their eyes bulging with madness, maybe fear...

The young men training to fly wore their polished boots and danced to ragtime, while Frenchmen in crayon-blue Paris-tailored uniforms came over with an eye patch or missing an arm or leg, to bring it all back. I just remember the songs we and the poor sods in the trenches hunting cooties in their shirts sang. We men in the air became more and more divorced from the murder of the infantry in hopeless battles. They sadly sang: "Take Me Back to Dear Old Blighty!" Romantic lyrics were gone. Now it was a flat statement:

> We're here because we're here
> Because we're here, because we're here...

Cocksmen sang:
> I love the ladies
> I love to be among the girls...

Airmen on leave found the old recruiting posters (and no longer fitting words in the song that went with them):

> Oh, we don't want to lose you,
> But we think you ought to go,
> For your King and Country
> Both need you so...

Out of tune with the young widows' black, the drunken whores found in London:

We shall want you and miss you
But with all your might and main
We will thank you, cheer you, kiss you,
When you come back again...

Songs like "My Buddy," and "The Rose of No Man's Land,"
made us want to puke. There was one song fliers sang getting
tanked up on whiskey, releasing pressures after losses on a raid.
I never saw it in print:

The young aviator lay dying
Beneath the wreck he lay.
These last parting words
To say:
"Take the cylinder out of my kidney,
The connecting rod out of my brain...
From my arse remove the crankshaft,
Assemble the fucking
Engine again!"

A Funny Way To Die

A Very Ordinary Story

Then I developed what I labeled "Goyas," something like
the feeling I got looking at Goya's etchings, the bad ones
of mad cats' eyes in the dark, and people being thrown into pits
full of cadavers. I'd come awake and there was no air in my
lungs; my teeth would be clicking together like knitting nee-
dles. I'd suck air and it was hard to get down, as if air had
become a solid. Then I'd feel my heart going at a fast clip—was
it ticking like a cheap tin alarm clock? All the time I'd have
trouble getting air down into my lungs, teeth still clicking
together, my arms and legs beginning to twitch. And I was
cold, very cold. The first times I had the Goyas, I took a suck
from the brandy and sat up the rest of the night wrapped in
two blankets, shivering, but getting some normal reactions to
my heart rate and my breathing. After three times of the

Goyas, brandy didn't work. Tony came in to my room, hearing me moving, and found me in a hell of a mess, a puddle of fear on the floor. He had me carried to the airfield hospital.

The medical sahib awakened and tut-tutting patted my arm. "A sort of anxiety seizure thing. Nothing vital to trouble me. Lots of it in Injuh. Get you to England to Sir Henry's hospital. That's his pitch, anxiety, nerves, that sort of balls-up."

So, I went to London on sick leave and attended special treatment in the clinic three mornings a week for my nerves, and not taking the pills Sir Henry the nerve wallah gave me. He, too, was an old fart from India. I was in no hurry to get back to flying.

I was supposed to live in, at a rest home for "war nerve cases." But I also had a bed-sitting-room on Oakley Street, Chelsea, and became intrigued by the way the people lived, drank, screwed, bitched between the "All Clear" and the next Alert.

One night at the Wheatsheaf pub, a tall blonde, in a long leather coat, impatient of the crush, asked me, "Would you be a love and get me a gin and lime? Can't get the bloody barmaid's attention."

I said of course. We had three each. Her name was Molly, her accent North of England. She was twenty, worked on invoices at the docks.

I felt I loved Molly like a swimmer loves a calm sea. That was after we went to the mat in my bed-sitter, making it while the gas ring fed by the shilling meter heated hot water for the toddies we drank, made with a fifth of bourbon I had gotten from a sailor.

Moll, as I called her, gave comfort and a great deal of feeling that life had value. I got a bigger bed-sitter on Charlotte Street among the pubs—we liked to make pub rounds. It was cozy.

Her stockings hung in the tiny bathroom and my pipes lay among her knickers, as I learned to call her drawers, and she called my suspenders braces, and my undershirt a vest. We liked to hole up when we were free, hid away in the room with the dusty blackout drapes, feeding on kippers and rashers of Irish bacon, a rare egg or two. Drink and roll around in the bed, stay there even when the bloody, ruddy Alert was on, not go down among the moldy, beery, shitty smells of drains and rot in the shelter by the greengrocer's.

Moll missed a period and then had a miscarriage. The Six Bells on King's Road was our hangout, and the Fitzroy, and we bought soldiers and the whores drinks. There were shows of course, *Chu Chin Chow* running forever—and a kind of fake gaiety on the posters and in the services that cheered up the reliefs home from France.

The English flier on leave or invalided home, recovering from a wound, watched his society changing, changing: so little like it had been when he was cheered and sent off to train on a flying field. He found much to drink, a great many partners, beds, games available. Always some fine-feathered lady giving a party for "the dear lads, poor chaps starved for the sight of a refined English woman." For some fliers there was a glimpse of home and family. But it was not calming. Still brooding on the front, on the dead fellow-airmen. It made them yearn for wilder ideas of pleasure, to go through the act of reproduction endlessly while still alive and kicking. With the right introductions and one's rank, one danced and made love in the houses of Lady A, Lady B, Lady C.

The rank and file on the other hand, had to make do with fish and chips fried in horse fat, weak beer, and when they were on rare leave for wounds, testing the tarts around Covent Garden or in Whitechapel. Or carrying a bag of French trash for Mum. Oh the sight of the ugly way of life, the kids so thin from blue-white milk, when they could get it, after standing two hours in line.

In bed with Moll, if the wind was right, we'd hear the far-away sound of the guns in France. It was good to feel warm and close to a clean body and think of the poor filthy sods in the trenches in the flogging rain and the mud. Also of the cold fog of the morning over the weedy airfield, the planes warming up, with stinking exhausts of blue smoke, and the fliers, hung over, tacky, sticky-eyed, climbing into foul flying gear... Bed was lovely.

It was a private London we made of it, Moll and me. The wartime city was all gloom—three years of war, maybe a million dead. A stalemate on the Western Front, donkey generals. There were night spots and drink and fine food for the rich and the red-tabbed staff officers and profiteers. But for the rest of them, a city of walking dead, every family focused on the casualty lists. Lights out, cold rooms, worn clothes. The Zeppelins were still coming over from time to time to drop bombs. One night, Moll and I, standing by the British Museum, saw one of the sausages. They followed the shiny Thames up to London. Saw this one caught in the searchlights. It began to smoke as a plane circled it with its incendiaries. A flame ran all along its back, and everything was on fire. It dipped and shivered and the cloth burned, was gone, so that the steel bones of it seemed cherry-red hot. It was falling. Then it was very dark again, just the ack-ack firing from the Putney marshes.

We held hands and went back to our place. I decided we'd get married; I suppose Herr Doktor Freud would say I had seen the failure of the biggest cock in the world as the symbol of something and was settling down. Truth was, I didn't want to go back to France and have nobody close by, caring, nobody to write silly letters to, and send me socks that didn't fit. Also I had come through all the young charge of the sex drive, and wanted a banking of the fires a bit. My nerves were rewired, in order again— but it was a patch job. I was looking for something less than full commitment, but for *something*. I still didn't like the word *love*, but what other one was there? I'd ask myself waking up, and Moll sleeping, smelling of woman, of night, of beer and of us.

Moll, when I said let's get married, said, "Oh, luv, it's no bloody time for it."

"No time is the right time."

"You're not the first, I mean not the luv I wanted. There was this chap I was walking out with. That was killed on the Somme. We didn't wait."

"Who cares?"

"There's the child, He's fifteen months."

"The chap's?"

"What the hell do you think luv! I was peddling arse along Piccadilly?"

I said no, I didn't think so at all. And the child was fine. A boy named for the chap, Chauncey, and staying with some folk in Kent on a farm.

So we set the wedding day and the nerve wallah at the hospital had me breathe into a paper bag, and touched my back with some fingers, asking me to guess "how many?" Sir Henry, the nerve doctor, was a little past his prime, but a good man for getting us crocks back in action. "I'd say two more weeks, and you'll be back in France. I'm not asking you to give up the drinking. Taper, taper off. But the blasted smoking..." He thumped my back. "Let me hear you cough. Yes, not so much smoking."

"I'm getting married."

He said he wished me and the future missus the best, and repeated two weeks for France "If they want you." I knew goddamn well they wanted me. The RAF was very short of fliers—losses were shocking—and old hands like me were valued above rubies.

On a Tuesday Moll went off to Kent to see Chauncey, and I had some of the last repairs done to my teeth that had to be done, leaving the more extensive work for later. We were to be married Friday, and one of the brass high in the RAF, with whom I had once flown, was going to see to it there was a party at Brown's, plenty of booze and the best food left in London. For all the misery and rationing and short supplies for the English (the damn U-boats were still sinking supply ships), you could—for a wink and a price—get Russian caviar, Danish suckling pig, the best French wines and a solid sirloin of beef from an Ireland busy raising good cattle and shooting at each other and the Black and Tans.

Life, of course—as you soon learn—is very cheap fiction. Life has no taste at all as to the proper way to do things. I mean I never found anything in Henry James or Stendahl that was an everyday way of how things are. No, life is trashy movies and cheap novels. Check your own life and prove how true I am.

Moll was killed, and the boy too, while riding in a milk cart in Kent; a lorry driven by a drunken, or sleepy, soldier crashed into them and mashed the life out of them against a stone wall.

You read about this sort of thing all the time during the war. War is very wasteful. I remember visiting a battle section and the rats so fat, they just couldn't eat another dead soldier...I'd tell myself it wasn't really love with Moll. Just being in London, and needing a woman in the kip. And being sloppy sentimental about it. But all the way back to the aerodrome in France, I knew I was fooling myself with a big lie. My trouble was I had become mature as I ever would be. I was no longer a callow boy, selling myself attitudes, poses. Maybe I was worse off. But whatever I was, I was different. I didn't carry Moll's picture on my body, or any letters. There were none. I've forgotten her, but my dreams, even now, don't seem to know that.

Living and Flying

So in time, by late 1917, I was flying. Being away from the aerodrome was like being homesick. There were usually four squadrons of us and two squadrons usually ate together. The enlisted men led a life of their own, the field having separate sleeping and eating quarters. A squadron needs two hundred enlisted men to be up to its quota, so eight hundred enlisted men hardly ever got into the air but serviced the planes, fliers, ground, and guns.

Medical officers ran a hospital unit, and there were stacks of raw-lumber coffins behind a building to bury the remains of recovered fliers. The infantry were buried where they fell—fliers usually got a ceremony in a real graveyard.

There were fuckups, of course. The cook and his staff stole, sold off part of the food supply. Alcohol, cigarettes, bedding, medical supplies, spare parts, dead fliers' gear, all sometimes had a way of being transformed into money or barter. Pilots' orderlies, batmen, old salts at looting, had the best of it, being boodle grabbers, all too close to the officers' food and whiskey.

Some small effort was made to camouflage aerodromes, but it hardly paid. Both sides knew where the major enemy fields were. Their only protection was antiaircraft fire from the guns that rimmed the field. Dugout shelters were handy. An alarm sent fighters into the air when enemy planes were reported approaching.

I did my part for the decor of the average officers' lounge. The remnants of enemy planes, such as propellers and insignia cut from wings; group photographs of fliers invalided home or dead; pictures of George V, the Kaiser, Woodrow Wilson, Mary Pickford, Fairbanks, and Charlie Chaplin. Notice boards and blackboards for flight orders, lots of dirty verse, pictures of nude or seminude women. Limericks so foul, the best always indecent, found pencilled or inked on latrine walls. The main room had collections of tattered old magazine and newspapers and usually a collection of novels, light or romantic, a frayed *Fanny Hill*.

Typical officer and private in conversation:

"Your bar bill, sir."

"Put it on the slate, Hughie."

"Major says slate got broken, sir."

"Fuck off, Hughie, and bring the whiskey."

"Righto, sir."

It was on the domestic bachelor side of living, unpaid tailor bills from London, letters, singly or tied in bundles, silver backed hairbrushes, splintered floors...

At first the aerodromes on the Western Front were a haphazard collection of tents and vans and cranky muslin planes kept on grass. Semipermanent fields were graded and rolled, favored a tarmac cover—tar and macadam rolled and pressed for a fairly smooth airstrip. Bomb craters could be quickly patched.

Night lighting was poor—often kerosene oil flares on oil barrels. Some planes carried Klaxons—auto horns; and air-to-ground sound signals—simple ones—were worked out.

By '17, an English aerodrome was usually set down near some town, one or two major roads passing through it. The flying area was a smoothed-out field, generally of sod with bare patches worn in it. Square or rectangular in shape, its four sides each about one-half to three-quarters of a mile long. It added up to our squadrons of planes, fighters, from eighty to ninety-five machines fit to fly, plus a junk pile of wrecked planes used for parts. Overnight the planes were kept in hangars; large sheds. Each hangar had room for a dozen machines and a mechanics' section for repairs and servicing. Three mechanics were assigned to each plane, mechanics filthy with oil stains, garments glossy with grease, their hands ingrained with worked-in grime. Near the hangars were the buildings that housed the flying officers and the mess halls.

"Just a jolly little world all our own," said the major.

I'll say this for the bloody British, they had class. "And as stiff with tradition as a weekend prick" (Chunky).

The upper classes usually attended a Church of England parade en masse; for them God was chiefly a state function. They had a certain air as fliers; the swagger stick, often an eyeglass, and a really shitty caste system—made up of the various grades of accents. Oxford and Cambridge on top, then stage actor's diction, Cockney H-droppers, Liverpool-Lancashire drone, the Scotts burr, the Australian twang, the Canadian drawl. Always accents decided one's social standing.

The food in the officers' mess was poor, unless we had a French cook and scrounged the countryside. One Frenchmen told me the British cuisine was "everything boiled to death in live steam, then covered with a white sauce made of wallpaper paste. Tea and tiffin are sacred chose jugée."

The French fliers on dress parade were impressive, but in

the main were given to slumpy ease, over-casual, clothes none too clean. Their view of events in the main, was cynical: "We know who is making a good thing out of it all back home, getting all the fine plump girls, drinking up the best wine." For their generals (fatras), contempt, for their political leaders, dirty suggestions. Most French fliers were Catholics, often pious, very anticlerical. I attended one Mass, it was a class approach to the Godhead rather than a spiritual one. He up there is *our* Boy. I made a note of the church service. Fat priest, broken ruin of a church, smell of soup cooking, church candles. A long line for confession. "Tomorrow we move up to the line."

I got away to London with René, this French flier, for six days. The usual grind of drink, snatch, hangovers—and, alas, clap. I went over to an American doctor for that, on getting back to France.

Everyone agreed that the most reckless, innocent, spendthrift with life were the Americans, those who joined the British and French air forces. All victims of myths of a lot of Buffalo Bill's Wild West Shows, Bronco Billy films, the tradition that as frontier folk, they were "half hoss, half alligator." A stomping, loud-mouthed folk, tall in the saddle and able to wrestle wildcats. Too many flew ignoring science and advice, and their casualties were fearful until they simmered down. "Often college men or students living abroad," the major said. Upper-middle-class spoiled sons full of pictures of planes, sure that it would be fun and romantic to fly in a war. It took time and tragedy, before they became good fliers.

In all the air forces, the main requirement was youth. Usually hastily trained, survivor of training crashes, along with the misfits, the unlucky, most weeded out by early death. Young men, some not yet shaving, with nothing but some coordination and a crazy desire to fly. I flew with a clerk, wastrel, cuckold, mechanic, actor, idler, cowboy, singer, shopkeeper, bugger, lawyer, virgin. Transfers from cavalry, infantry, sports, and a few from the Church.

The longer the war lasted, the more I noticed I was losing my usual desire to fuck. I just didn't wake up horny, no welcoming hardons. In time, I felt cunt the most overrated item in the world. I found out it happened to lots of fliers after a while; on leave, they couldn't even get it up for their wives.

There were English and French officers—even some who were aces, who on leave dressed in gowns and painted up as women and battled the Paris flics—these murderous sissies hating to put away their wigs and evening gowns. Old generals came to us to talk up the Allied War Drives. In Berlin, we were told, the beer cellars echoed to the songs of fliers who dreaded to sleep and lived on brandy and milk and talked. Of what? Die Todten reiten schnell, and Kurvenkampf flying.

One day a German Albatross pilot, his head, I suppose, stuffed full of German glory-and-horseshit, Wagner and Nietzsche, dropped the boots of a dead Allied ace over his home aerodrome and no one fired a shot. It was the last of the old-fashioned wars—if you didn't have to live in the trenches, or do the retreat from Mons; lie there, as I saw it at a dressing station, screaming, your entrails in your hand.

We fliers vomited our cognac-and-coffee breakfasts over the instrument panel as we banked our muslin birds, trying to get an advantage or avoid the machine guns of the Richthofen Circus blazing into our blind spot. Somehow at home in the newspapers it all came out as knighthood and tournaments in the stories being written about us. When my dreams are bad, I still smell the fur-lined leather coats, feel the great goggles on our eyes (like the look of goldfish in a bowl), a flutter of scarf around a cold neck, ends flowing in the wind from the helmet top like a bit of Sung drapery...a throat full of bile. That was how it was flying that war...

After Chunky and six others in two days went down in flames with nothing left to bury, flying became a horror to us old crocks. We were soon, we were told, going to be withdrawn from the advance aerodromes. By mid-1918, as we drank our café marc and waited, the war increased in rumor, fury, headlines. I was leading young English fliers who hardly seemed to understand the theory of it, while the Germans were in as bad a way too, desperately sending staffels of twelve machines out against every patrol, using the Halberstadt fighter to good advantage—a machine that pulled up in a loop so fast we seemed to be walking.

I'd come in from patrol, goggled eyes still full of pirouetting burning planes, and the dirty dusty fields of summer where we were stationed still within sound of the front where the Americans were moving up under their tin hats, faces like the ones I once knew at home in high school. I felt like yelling, "What goddamn craziness brought you stupid shitheels here?"

After the Americans set up their air force units, I'd go visiting them. But I didn't feel any kinship to these pink-faced kids with their Mr. Zip short hair cuts and clean teeth. I was in 1918 twenty years old, felt a hundred and ten—and didn't want to hear their cheerful crap about "hanging Kaiser Bill from a Sour Apple Tree." I could have transferred to a USA unit, but didn't.

Over in France, after delays and problems, squadrons like the 95th had a kicking mule as its insignia, Maude the Mule from the comic strip, also a song, "Hurrah for the Next Man to Die." For a kill in the air, the winner had to treat the company; downing an enemy plane rated five bottles of champagne; getting downed yourself, three bottles; cracking up on landing, one bottle. That and learning to say "Mercy boocoo" and "vin rouge," and a few direct needed dirty questions were the first lessons. One flier told me, "It's fine to hear the French girls yelling Vivent les Américains! Vive Pershing! Vivent les États-Unis!"

American infantry went by in camions and the fliers yelled out, "Give the squareheads hell!" One doughboy yelled back, "Fuck you."

There was entertainment for fliers and infantrymen. Not all the doughnuts and coffee were free. Some USA organization made a good cash balance out of entertaining the boys; but the runners who carried doughnuts up to the front could be proud to report: "We never lost a doughnut." It was all so depressing—because these kids were like me, John, Chunky, in 1915. And I was an old-young man and their doughnuts gave me a toothache.

Yes, yes, America had been sucked into the war. Oh, my grandmother's balls how the USA had been sucked in. Everybody at the field who could get drunk, got drunk, even the fliers going out on patrol. The older ground officers saw American guns, planes, dollars, lots of lovely dollars. They asked me about American whiskey, "Bourbon, I believe you chaps call it." I said it was a skull cracker. We all stood up and drank at mess to the King, to the President, to victory. Until the batmen had to take most of us off to bed…

When they came to fly, they were a special lot, these Americans, in their mooncalf innocence of European ways. They were overreckless in an already faded frontier tradition of the face-off and the quick draw. They flew with daring and many did not last long in the air. No matter how wild their habits grew, they had a puritanical sense of duty our major said—and only at the end "knew the sad impermanence of all actions." They ran to extremes; they were either better, or more keyed up, than the average man under delicate, split-second, deadly conditions. Most had a driving adolescent dependence on the seeking out of action and excitement.

In their frenzy, they sure retained an American contact with their country, town, city, street upbringings; even if somewhat battered at times. They remained full of American ideals much longer than I had. In the air, as they put on the rudder without banking, or took on a Jagdstaffel of fast interceptors, they often, I was sure, mistook themselves for settlers holding off red hostiles or riding shotgun on the Overland Stage. Often short lives, transient joys, were their destiny. Few of them understood the true failure and agony, the asshole of a Europe they fought to

save or serve. All lived vaguely in hope of some greater good
to come; none could put together with any sense words that
explained their actions or themselves.

On Brandy and Milk

For a while John was sent to the Italian front. His letters were good stuff and I kept them. He seemed to like the life and there were times, when my tail was dragging on the ground, I wished I were there with him.

Most daring bastards in the world, the Wop fliers, crazy for the girls, the vino bianco, and the gramophone records of *Trovatore*. Good friends and full of gestures. Always crossing themselves, wearing saints' medals, mocking the priests and the Pope. Much contempt for the peasants. The gents are lazy, bone lazy, but grand in their uniforms and scented like a Kansas City whore. They fly crazy and with dash and a smile... And wave to you, 'ello, paesano. Off duty they brag about their flying, play caffe-biliardo in the cafes, and the young tenentes go off to the brothels. They sure come back full of grappa and are very polite and laugh too much. They all invite you to visit their parents in Rome, or some hill vineyard after the war. Two or three die every week. The wounded, when recovering, look at you with those big black eyes and ask you is it truly a dreadful wound.

The chow is not bad. Veal, pasta, Piccioni arrosto, if you're a soto tenente or soto colonello, what I think are robin red breasts, and pasta—Jayus, the pasta and the garlic. But the strega and the grappa will kill anything on your breath.

The dago generals are even worse than our chowderheads. They have been taking a real beating. Everybody ran in the big retreat, and they kept shooting their own rank and file as a lesson. I don't know as how we can really do much here. The Austrians are very good up there in the mountains, and the Italian fliers are very bad, tell the truth. I wouldn't give fifty lira for their chances against some of the Heinie Jagdstaffels on the Western Front. The quim smells of olive oil and she crosses herself after you shuck your pants, and says "a vostro beneplacito."

I shall soon be back in France (somewhere in) as they say in the newspapers. We'll get jolly and talk about us living it up in Rome after the war. What do you hear from your folks?

Ciao

John.

As for me, I didn't shoot off my mouth. I was developing British phlegm and secret grievances.

Tony, who had grown melancholy at missing women, and

played all day on a gramophone a recording of Shubert's, taught me a bit of Yiddish and took up the violin which he played well but in a gloomy manner. I was happy when John came back.

John was flying in a unit fifty miles up the line with the dog Fritz he had inherited when Chunky went, as his only companion in the cockpit. John had threatened his C.O. with a Very pistol cartridge up his arse when the C.O. tried to force on the squadron a plane with elevator controls the factories had put in wrong.

John wrote me in a letter I still have: "It's a very starchy war for our Limeys, but you get up there among the cumulus clouds in an FE2 with the 250hp. Rolls-Royce engine and they can keep the old crazy worn-down earth. There's a whole universe unused. Say, you long-haired bastard, you ever read *Faust*? 'We fear the blows we never get. And those things we never lose, is what we lament.' Damn good for a Heinie. Faust differs from all other intellectuals in that he hunted experience under skirts through hooch—besides knowledge. To hold life in total vision is damn hard. If we can get poor Chunky's auto working, we'll come down maybe to your field soon with some native fellows we've been bunking with, of the 12ième Groupe d'Escadrilles de la Chasse, the French élite squadron. Only we call them Storks. I'm in a bad way, as the poet Hafiz said, 'Who can't drink, can't love.' I've got an ulcer, the Doc thinks. No letter from Sue, who is now some place in the Near East with the Red Cross. I don't know anything much that's true. I'm scared."

That set me back on my heels a bit, solid John cracking.

Tony and I were taking up a wing of twelve. The trouble was that usually there was a strong wind from the west, so that if we took our sucklings, just out of solo school, too far over the German lines and a dog fight broke us up, they'd drift so far east in their excitement they'd never have the petrol to make it back. They were all as eager as bridegrooms who had read all about screwing in a book. But green, green, green.

The Germans had their Aviatik two-seaters out, and we had no back-up at all in the air except from the Escadrille Lafayette at Bar-le-Duc. We didn't get on too well with them. They had been the Escadrille Américaine, N. 124, flying the Vosge sector. They felt it was not playing the old ball game for Tony and me to be flying with the lousy Limeys when we could fly with them, real solid American he-men, who were going into the Hat-in-the-Ring group, USA. But they could fly, and could die, who couldn't? Dying? People do it all the time.

Tony in his flying pants, unshaved, eyes bloodshot, was to fly wing for me and the sucklings. The planes snorted and stank on the flying field, hustling at their wheel blocks, the castor oil a fearful odor, blue smoke tossing pebbles among the dying weeds. I got in my crate, raised my hand in the saddle, and we took off into the rising day, bluish shadows in the plane trees we just got over, the air warm as English beer, the day still dark to the east.

The sun was slanting on our left as we wheeled up and up in case the staffel of the late Herr Immelmann were in a kill-kill mood and were hunting our ass. I let the airstream clear my head. I hoped to endure, with care. I was living on coffee, raw eggs, and brandy again, and any day I hoped to hear the major say I'd been elevated out of combat and could go to a nice rest in London. Bathe, see a doctor again about my nerves, get more teeth fixed, read a book...I had no sex desires left at all. It didn't even bother me that I didn't want to prong a woman anymore. It was at the time I was acting like I were crazy for the doctors— and I knew it was an act and they said I only thought it was an act when I confessed...

Tony was wagging his wing. To the far left I saw were a herd of Drachen, German kite balloons up to observe and direct artillery fire. I signaled no. We had to ride a contact patrol with some land action. And the Drachen were protected by nasty AA fire, and Boche pilots lurked someplace in the clouds nearby to take care of the foolish fighter who was sucked in by balloons.

I gave my Lewis guns a burst to clear them for action. They often jammed. I was thinking that this horse's nuts air fighting we were doing had no real military value; merely anonymous butchery that the press wrote up. When *zam!* we walked right into it. The clouds having drifted away, we were blinded by the sun. In two layers, red painted triplane Fokkers were down on us; black crosses and mean. They had been stacked just above the cloud bank. My sucklings ganged up like fox-nervous hens. I dumped my retrospective thoughts, kicked the rudder, went into a roll, saw the babies under my wing try and follow. Tony pulled up in a loop, always a crazy fine flier, and he came around and to the left, firing in bursts. A red-nosed Boche went down and around, wind screaming like a fury through his wires.

A dogfight is a rocketing chaos; chasing tails I had enough to do. Some of the Huns' new planes were firing one-pound pom-poms. I saw one of my babies go crazy, wobble in a tailspin, pour black smoke and come apart. I suppose he forgot his belt for he fell out screaming, but I was in trouble myself. I put on rudder without banking. I had two enemies, one above me, and the one below in the blind spot was pumping slugs into me. I could feel canvas and wood splinter and tear and I prayed oh-shitandpiss, if I get it now, give it to me a fast one right through my brain or heart, as I gave a few of them. No burning, no burning, no falling, falling to mash into a field. ("He fell at dawn on a clear quiet day.") I kept the trigger finger ready, and kicked up and let the top Hun feel my guns. I let go half a drum, twenty-four rounds, but he ate it all, and I knew it wasn't my day. I jabbed at the rudder bar, pushed the stick over and went into a steep dive. But they followed me down. The unshaved bastard behind his goggled eyes was staring at me. I panicked, my asshole went tight, but my deep inner survival nerves—they didn't give a ticker's itch about my surface ones—they told me what to do and how to do it.

I took a quick look in the blue quadrangle of sky. My flight had blown apart. Some of my babies were scattered, or falling burning or breaking up. Tony—I hunted his ship—he had a thumb-on-nose insignia painted on his fuselage. He was flying far below, near the treetops, dodging three Heinies on his tail, trying to lure them low enough to crash them into the ground. I didn't see more. I was off to the north and they east—the horizon spinning like a fever dream—trying to get clear. One bastard clung just below in the blind zone, and I knew if I kept up going east, I'd run into Jadgstaffel interceptors.

I poured on coal to get a black exhaust, suddenly stalled and went down tail first, hoping I could get out of it in time. The Hun shot out in front of me. I came out of the dive, roared up and around and over him. I fired the rest of the drum, put in another drum (try it sometimes if you ever find an old Camel in a museum), working stick, rudder, elevator controls, feeling the oil gauge drop—one hand loading, wind tearing at you, the Hun circling to get behind and below.

And he had me. My motor sounded like a grease-spitting iron skillet frying flounders.

It's marvelous for your nerves, dying in a damn bright sun. Makes you think, repent, shrinks your scrotum. I could feel the plane shudder as he fired short bursts, but lots of them. Then there was the sound of a Klaxon (we carried them to signal ground patrols) and a big blue fighter with English oval insignia was to the left of us. It had two fixed Vickers guns firing through the air screw, and the Hun just went up into an exploding rose. Breaking at once into fragments. The blue Nieuport wagged its wings. I made a feeble bless-you-kind-stranger gesture of thanks—held my hands in prayer position. Then it was that I felt my right leg and hip burn, and I put down a glove furtively to investigate. It came up smeared with black blood. Funny, I hadn't felt it during my funk. I gave a curdled smile. Was I dead or out of the war? Worm meat, or London on a cane?

I didn't think I could make it back to the field, so I began to look for a place to bring down my ruptured duck, oil spitting in my face. I couldn't work the rudder, so I used the tail surface for some kind of wearing around, and the engine was hot. I couldn't see, the goggles were smeared. I pulled them off. It was a fun day and I didn't want to bleed to death at two thousand feet. Tony kept above me on guard, and I came down hard—too hard—in the frontline trenches of a Canadian outfit. The Princess Pats. A colonel with the ADC said it was a damn improper landing when they brought me through the wire. I smiled and said, "That's right."

I passed out there and woke up in a hospital with a little New York City doctor shouting: "Beautiful, beautiful. It's a hip wonderful to work on. Give the povero diavolo another whiff of ether, Miss Dreamboat." I fell down into happiness and quoted Buddha to myself: "The sword follows space without exertion to the wound." I felt good. The war was over for me. I was a human being again. I hoped the wonderful wop didn't take off the leg; my last thought was, how embarrassing to get into bed with a woman with my leg off—*sorry baby, this is all of me.* The ether sang and the most important thing I ever learned filled my head. Survival is all...

Paris From Below

The City of Light

It was the summer of 1919 when they finally let me out of the London bone-healing hospital for war cases, saying my hip was as good, or bad, as it would ever be now or later. Which meant I had one of those dignified slight limps and my cane, if thin enough, gave me the air of one solid sonofabitch who had lived through the world war, and had the scars to show for it—when he dropped his duds. There had been complications, infections, bits of bone coming through the scar tissue. Months and months—nearly a year of it. But I was alive and had a pittance of a disability allowance as a damaged RAF ex-officer, I think seven dollars a month. And that stopped after a year or so for reasons that only Parliament could figure out, and some ex-officers went broke as chicken farmers or became sidewalk chalk artists or buskers. I had two French decorations, and an

Italian one (red and green), what for, I don't know, and three British items.

Most of all I had a touch of wonder about the future; only a touch. I was twenty-one, rangy, tall, too thin—but gaining weight. Had color from sitting on the sun terrace of the hospital, in between the medical students picking bone fragments out of my prat.

I had a lot of blank white space in my mind. I wasn't thinking back about the war. I wasn't interested in the peace they were patching up. I had no trust in leaders or diplomats—ever notice their mouths all look like rectums? My last illusions had been shot down with Chunky and other comrades. I would remain in the human race; I had to, it wasn't like a club from which you could resign... But I wasn't going to hug it close, or trust it. As my grandfather had once put it, "The only sensible thing to do on a sinking ship is to take a warm bath."

Unlike what came to be called "the lost generation" (and soon one couldn't avoid them in Paris, or in Greenwich Village), I lacked their romantic bullshit in my makeup that set them in an aspic of self-pity and drink, made art or a replica of some avant-garde ritual out of their little hurts gotten between 1914 and 1918. Maybe I escaped because I didn't want to be a writer, a poet, or a painter, not even compose music.

I didn't want to go home. My grandmother was dead, and my grandfather was becoming a bit potty; he thought stamp collecting the height of human reason. If I could get one of the family trusts to give me a little bit of money every month, I decided I'd stay on in Europe. Chunky was dead, shot out of the air like a mallard in hunting season. John, the other boy I had gone to Canada with and into the RFC (later the RAF) was in Rome. Writing me to come on down. It sounded good, the vino and the big city and the garlic and olive oil smell of the girls, and the cheapness of living at the exchange rate. But then later Mussolini and his gang took over, and I decided no, I'd try Paris.

There was this Englishman, Whitey, built low to the ground, a big smile, over-life-sized teeth and not an H to his name. He had flown with me in the war and married a French war widow. A young, wide, pretty one from the snapshot he sent me. He was running a garage and petrol station in Clichy. He was good with engines and had during 1918 often kept our flying coffins in the air with baling wire and spit.

Early in 1920, exploiting old friendship, I was living in their domicile fixe, a nice enough flat over the garage, rooms smelling of auto grease and Babette's cooking, which was not Norman peasant cuisine but really gourmet chow and very filling.

It was for Europe a time of garrulous politicians and no one sure civilization had survived; in the bistros and cafés, after two bocks, you started worrying about civilization and the high cost of living.

Whitey was doing pretty well, good with the garage, the gas, and handling a line of Michelin tires and some special kind of spark plugs. Babette made him a good wife. She was broad of beam as a good dray horse, and had a high color, high cheekbones, and tied little blue ribbons into her mustard-colored hair. She was practical, frugal, and when angry let Whitey have it in a fast Normandy jargon which neither of us could figure out too well, laced with Paris curses à la "un sale youpin!"

"She needs a set of knuckles in 'er ear," Whitey would say as he bent over the entrails of some motor car while Babby stood facing us in her petticoat, with stockingless legs, her hair done up in a bun. She'd wave a dish cloth at him and shout, "Fool de mauvais augure." It seemed Whitey was giving credit to old war buddies for petrol.

"Shut your 'ole, dearie, or you'll be 'aving to pick up your teeth."

"Maquereaux!"

They really loved each other, and Babby was fine when she could take over and count the tattered franc notes and the worn coins, nod, and that's the last Whitey saw of them. Babby paid the bills, signed the orders. They were trying to make a baby and I'd go out and walk around among the femmes honnêtes and les bas fonds that infected the district. I didn't think it was polite to stay and listen to Babby coming in the big mahogany bed she and Whitey filled. They had bodies like Percheron horses. She really had orgasms that sounded like the death scene of a prima donna in an opera cutting loose with all she's got in a final aria.

I was getting some of my own back on the old sex road. What with the cuisine bourgeoise at Whitey's—eggs, mayonnaise, coxhonnailel Auvergne, poulet de Bresse, country butter. I was letting out to new notches in my belt. I did draw the line at cooked ortolans and tripe.

I began to take on Paris, 1920, like an overcoat—sort of wear the city. There were two Dutch sisters, nice, blonde, full of frivolity, Anneke and Domela van O——, who managed a photo studio and camera supply shop in Montparnasse. They had original sketches by Van Dongen and Pascin on a wall. They were not whores, and Annie was engaged to a policeman named Hilaire, a bike flic from the 14th Arrondissement, a big burly fellow who used to ride in the professional bicycle races with Flaminck the painter. Sundays, we four, we'd pack a basket and go up river and at a boat café get the sisters a vin blanc cassis, or a café aerose rhum, and we'd stick to Calvados. Then to find a bosky riverbank, drink wine and eat out of the basket, open our flies and loosen our belts, and the girls would piddle in the bushes and take off shoes and stockings. We'd all take a snooze to come awake to a fine blue sky and green trees. So we'd do a little or a lot of riverbank screwing. Nobody caring, as "that's what the riverbanks are made for," said the innkeeper where we went for supper.

Usually we had a soufflé à l'Armagnac, ending with a fromage de chèvre, and drinking Gevrey-Chambertin (I'm recording all this to needle Ernest who likes these kinds of inventories of feeding and drinking). It was all very good and enjoyable, and Hilaire would recite Racine. Pretty good for a cop: "Le bonheur semble fait pour être partagé."

Back to the sisters' place and we'd make it all night, Hilaire getting up at five in his not-too-clean long underwear, to go ride his bike to his morning post. Anneke and Domela yawning awake later, rumpled and scratching and laughing, turning me out at seven as they had to open up the shop. Sometimes we were a little late because of a morning quickie or two. The sisters were always willing and jolly, and it was like copulating with a couple of Reubens, when the old man was at his feisty best painting fat girls.

It all ended when Hilaire married a rich widow with a pork shop near the Café Zeyer. The sisters went out to Java to run a hotel there for coffee planters. For some time I got postal cards from Batavia; Surabaja, with nice stamps, then nothing.

Whitey was arrested for some kind of a deal in stolen Italian motor parts. I never did get the full facts. He and Babby went to Nice after somebody high up was paid off. They ran a taxi service on the Riviera, and had four babies in three years. They became stuffy and very respectable, and sent me Christmas photos of their daughters in their churchgoing best white. Whitey didn't even think I was a good risk to lend money to—at a time when I was trying to get the family trust to be more generous with me.

My Hungarian Wife

I wanted a good simple life, nothing to bug me—no job, wife, babies, politics, causes. I read a lot, sat in cafés, parks, visited sites of interest—no museums or churches, but race tracks, sports events, film shows, river trips. By 1922, I was living in a hotel on the Rue Bonaparte, and by that time the Americans were coming in hordes—like jolly carnivora—ducking the Citroen horns, happy in the cafés and estaminets, posing for Kodak pictures behind the Louvre in the Luxembourg Gardens. All gussied up in clean pressed clothes. They would inch up to you and ask you how was Paris and how did one get to know it, how to meet the loafers and the flâneurs, who were the people *there*—were they famous?—boozing or taking coffee at the Dôme, the Rotonde. Were they the real stuff—artists, writers—that kind of thing?

Damned if I knew or cared. I came to know Elliot Paul very

well. He was to get involved with *transition*, and I remember Otto Kahn in Paris, and Charlie Chaplin, Douglas Fairbanks, Mary Pickford and Adolph Menjou, also the American Legion bums cavorting.

I belonged with the Americans settled in Paris, who didn't get into the memoirs. Just untalented ordinary citizens, businessmen, below-stairs people, and the high-pocket crowd from the American Embassy. Department-store buyers, embezzlers, fugitives, engineers, graves identification people searching for the AEF who died for France and England. I met some pathetic relics of the Edith Wharton-Berry Wall Paris, lost without Henry James.

We unimportant, inartistic Americans were a large group, maybe forty, fifty thousand of us in Paris. Americans more or less well-heeled or just making it. The rate of exchange was a dilly for us. Yet in the last few years, most people think about fifty Americans who wrote about each other, were the only ones living there. Sinclair Lewis drunk, e. e. cummings ("Waiter, make me a child, so this is Paris"). Dos Passos losing his glasses. Hart Crane, arrested for slugging, kicking waiters, trying to sneak a punch at a flic. They caused a lot of talk.

I was in the Paris clink myself, at the invitation of the Sûreté Général, twice, and so were a few other nonartistic Americans, and no one wrote about it.

My police problems were not serious. A fight with a hotelkeeper over a typewriter I'm sure he swiped. The other time was when I tried to help a couple of South Americans, fun seekers, homosexuals, who were being beaten up and robbed off the Rue de l'Odéon on the Left Bank. The flics arrested *me*, not the hoodlums who ran for it, and I ended up at the Ile de la Cité. However, I knew this State Department fairy at the American Embassy—greatly interested in the behinds of waiters—and he knew Cocteau and Gide and Candel, and so it was fixed up. I came out of the French clink with just a few fleas and a sense of how right Daumier was about the failure of justice in French courts.

I got married. Her name was Etelka Horvath—but was called Sari by all—or as they put it in Hungarian, Horvath Etelka, a dancer at Zelli's who drank coffee with chickory before a meal. I met her at a party Ford Madox Ford gave. People are more vulnerable at parties. Ford was always giving parties, and talking up young writers I didn't want to read or hear about. It was a fine short marriage of eerie domestic life. I learned to curse in Hungarian, a very difficult language and we never fucked at all; no bacchanalian byplays or games either. It seems, she told me, she had a great dislike of sex, having been deflowered by a Grand Duke Andrassy, the son of someone close to Franz Josef. It was all a lie, of course—Hungarians lie a lot, Sari told me. And everybody calls Magyar girls Sari in Paris, even if their name is Etelka—she told me—yoi ishtanem—Hungarians lie from birth. "Sari is a better name than Mitzi, which is the second favorite name for Hungarian girls." The fag at the embassy had arranged our wedding, made it easy, cut the red tape. He had warned me, "The little bitch, she may only want to be a US citizen."

I said, "Teh briluend," which is Hungarian for "you creep."

I was water, I was putty in Sari's hands. I think it was the last carry-over of my war madness, uncoordinated nerve shakes. Feigned or real, I did still have something, a trace of it caught in the war. And Sari was the last symptom of it.

She had red-gold hair, a Sung-vase china-white skin (I'm quoting Elliot Paul on this point) and one of those teasing voices, a bit coarse but liquid. She moved her head like a metronome when excited. I didn't think she married me to get to the United States. I suspected she just wanted to stay off the streets. She was in that in-between state of being a whore and not being a whore. She still couldn't see ass-peddling as a full-time profession. I was maybe to be the transmission belt. As for not wanting it to be sex between us, later, much later, I came around to thinking she wanted me to beat her first, brutalize her, rape her, choke her, or worse. A goddamn masochist. I remember when

I was a boy living in my grandfather's town, the mill hands, "Hun-kies" they were called, Mittel-European peasant, always beat their wives on payday, the women expected it; if no beating, they sus-pected he was unfaithful. I didn't know. Oh, I slapped her twice. I even knocked her off a chair at the Dôme one night. None of it, however, was sensual. I didn't press the screwing issue, being a decent American boy who asked permission; is the pubic wel-come mat out? After two months of this face-off, some big Hun-garian named Geza showed up and said Etelka—Sari—Mitzi—was his wife and had run off and he had now found her, and now wanted her. There were two children back in Buda and Pest. He slapped her face hard, back and forth like a baker getting a loaf ready for the oven. She smiled. Was delighted. So all I got out of it was to find out Budapest was really two cities sep-arated by the Danube. I tell it all so easy, but I was shaken up by it. I wasn't a European yet.

I liked Paris. There were even a few French men and women I liked and got to know well. Few Americans did that. I mean know the real middle class; teachers, engineers, doctors, brick-layers, wholesale market people, government clerks that ran "le gouvernement français." Even the misfits of the Rue Château Landon I liked. Mostly, I liked my life. Easy, placid, almost flow-ing like water, no channel it had to follow, and going around obstacles because I couldn't be bothered to make duties for myself. I suppose I was wary, even scared of having to go into the "Ou Ess Aye" family mills and plants ("nephew of our president—treat him like anyone else"), of having to sit in any office, sign invoices, and talk about the percentage of the national product we would try to grab off.

With this kind of thinking, I admit I did fit in with the Amer-ican writers and painters and arty loafers, not wanting too close a smell of rich materialism. Shitheads like Harding, and then Coolidge, didn't seem to impress us sensitive delicate natures (ha, ha) as being worthy to represent or understand us. We would only return to see if we could screw some more cash or check allowances out of our families to keep us in Paris. I went back for that reason.

Americans visiting Paris get excited over simple things. Like peeing in public streets. No Frenchmen makes a fuss about using those little structures where, duty done, he comes out buttoning his fly as he walks along.

But a tourist came to me with an item from the press, "The male comfort station, the pissotière, they say, will soon go. I've been looking forward to giving one a try. Do you have a favorite?"

"Well, they're not gone yet."

The pissotière is a realistic monument of the Paris streets. A simple architectural need in ironwork by the Voierie. It hides little for what is serves—the relief of taking a leak. It has a rich odor—like the stables of our boyhood. It came in—in cast iron—in the 1890s. Paris landscape artists added it to their paintings. My favorite is the one by the Bibliotheque National, next a beaut outside Notre Dame. The drone of Latin in an atmosphere of ammonia, monks-cloth, and pious flies. The Bourse pissotière is too busy, the Morgue's leak-tower is rusty, the cemetery ones depressing. The Pantheon has two, overrun by fairies offering tidbits and services.

To American Legion visitors, I'd point out the stations at the Porte de Montreuil, Porte des Lilas, Porte de Clignancourt—all had their pissoirs. Elliot Paul favors the Boulevard Voltaire spots. Ernest talked of the rough trade, the gavroche, the pimp, the apache, the cocher, and the bike riders and boxers of the spot near the Moulin de la Galette. They come in all sizes, shapes, the shed, the cylinder, also neoclassic Art Nouveau. Scott, who always hid his tool with a hand in a pissoir, once said, "I'm buying one for Max Perkins, my editor at Scribner's—he can raise flowers in it."

After Sari was dragged back to Budapest (by her hair, I hoped), I moved in with Russell R——. I suppose you've seen Russ a hundred times, and never bothered to find out about him. Russ played piano discreetly during cocktail hours, performed in little supper joints, noodled the keys in ratty night clubs after hours, played old favorites while you drank, or got set up for the night. Stephen Foster, Irving Berlin, Victor Herbert, Russ neat in his blue-green aged tux, large bow tie, curly hair held down by grease, pinky ring showing a blue glass stone. He could play anything you asked for: "Muskrat Ramble," "Boola Boola," "St. Louis Woman," "Melancholy Baby," "Beautiful Ohio," "Blood on the Saddle," "My Gal Sal." He had this marvelous musical memory, and if you could hum, he could fake it. Americans in Paris asked often for Jolson's songs, also "Pony Boy," and "Silver Threads Among the Gold."

Russ had done the New York speaks, and the London cellar dives where titled folk and nance playwrights slumming dropped coins or notes into the large brandy glass Russ kept on the piano and salted with some five-dollar bill, pound note, or ten francs. The Riviera, the Lido, Hamburg helling spots at some time or other had Russ seated under a soft light in some corner at a piano. Playing cocktail hour music, supper music, late-owl tunes. Russ was from a good solid Virginia family: "Tobacco farmers, horse breeder, hunters—shit like that. I was the freak—I liked to read." Russ was a pleasant roommate. Very well educated. I stole a couple of volumes of his Pepys' journals, which he had swiped from a British poet and fairy he had been living with the year before.

I had never lived with a homosexual roommate before. Had only accepted the arrangement on a nonsexual agreement because I had been playing the horses and was very low in funds—needed shelter during a very cold and rainy season.

Russ never laid a finger on me and I could turn my back on him with safety. We had our separate social hours arranged. I'd bring a girl in during the hours he played from five to one in the morning, at some place near the Scheherazade or Ciro's. He had the boys in from ten in the morning to three in the afternoon, when I was sitting in the parks, making the rounds of the cafés, window shopping Yendis or Guérins, spitting like a philosopher into the river from some of the six or seven bridges, my favorites the cast-iron bridge structure and the one with the big stone soldiers with their boots in the water if the season was in flood.

I had decided to stay in Paris if I could manage it. I didn't want to win any rat race back home; because even if you won, what were you? A rat. That's why they called it a rat race—non?

The American sissy world in Paris is no more interesting than any place else, only in Paris it's safer. Very bitchy, catty, pouting, rather mean when angry and good fun when in their cups or in love. The love affairs never lasted for long—and were mostly out in the open. From the USA came writers, actors, hairdressers, art critics, composers, museum staffers, chorus boys, young vicars, priests, embassy and state department crews to feel free to offer a boy Dry Monopole, or a pinch on the cheek.

Americans are so caught up in New England ideas of morals and a sense of guilt, they never open their eyes all the way.

The sissy world is often love for one-night stands, quick pick-ups in the bars featuring feathered pink lampshades. Some couples did settle in, a few settling for a couple of weeks—that was almost a marriage.

I never objected much to what went on. It wasn't to my taste, but not on moral grounds—if this is what they liked, this is what they liked. As long as they didn't bugger boys under twelve, or try and suck your cock unasked at a party, they could live in their versions of a tacky world free of any feeling. I never gave a damn. A lot of young male whores and painted imps did a good class of business in blackmail of Americans. And there were some threats of acid flinging over who owned W. H. and R. N., the Hollywood actors. The fags were dreadfully cruel to each other at times. And ready to weep on your shoulder and offering to paint your fingernails or do the housework.

Russ kept tabs on the doings around town. A lot of Americans, best-selling authors, a composer or two are usually fagging it in Paris. One or two Book-of-the-Month-Clubbers I have had to help onto the boat at times, crying out, "Russell dear, would you see that Raoul or Rene or Dodo don't get into trouble."

Dodo, I knew, had a wife and three kids he was peddling his rump to support. And that Rene runs a discreet house off Rue Madame, where clergy of many denominations arriving from America could be introduced to plump little choirboys.

If I was at first shocked at all this—and I don't think I was—I accepted it. Like war, legal executions, strike-breaking, Tea Pot Dome, the Bolshies in Russia murdering each other, all as the way the world had decided to play the game. Yet I knew marvelously simple people, decent middle-class people on the Rue du Cardinal-Lemoine, and some rich who had a sense of humor and lots of Château Rausan Gassies, and knew they had the best of it. Even in Paris there were loyal husbands, faithful wives, obedient children. Even charity and kindness, not merely on Sundays or holidays.

But all these were a minority, as it must be every place. So, for me, the life of Russ and his crackling, bitching, buggering world was just something that was there, as he played "Ramona" and "Three O'Clock in the Morning" for the cocktail and nightbird trade.

Russ was getting more and more excited. Not over a love affair; he was working up an act for the music halls or vaudeville. "I can't stand the cocktail-hour supper-music pace anymore. I've met this woman, Lotte, she's a friend of Adrienne Monnier. She plays the violin and we're working out a musical novelty act. Nothing like it ever been done. Keith Circuit in New York will be interested." I met Lotte at La Maison des Amies des Livres.

Lotte was a good bit bigger than Russ. She had a heavy torso and muscled legs. She worked out with barbells, she told me. I'm no judge of music—I have a stone ear—so I don't know if what Lotte and Russ practiced was any good. Popular stuff with zing, and Brahms, Rimsky-Korsakov, near classics—the two of them bowing and banging along. Then suddenly they were off to London to show the act to someone who was "just crackers about it."

Luckily I had a good run with the horses; I had found a Longchamps paddock worker who would go shares from time to time. If I bet—bought some tickets—he'd tell me of a race that—with a wink—was "*very* likely." So I moved away from the sissy world.

As for Russ and Lotte, just about a year ago, I was near Mesnil-Theribus, and there was this shabby little theater, or music hall, painted electric blue, RUSSEL et LOTTE EN HAUT! I wish I hadn't gone in. The act wasn't too bad among the dancing dogs, a molting clown, a strong man with loose dentures. The music they made was delightful enough and Lotte in an evening gown looked like a refugee from a Wagnerian opera, the cherry-colored violin almost lost under her massive chin. Russ was always a good piano player with style, and he did the stuff with feeling, Tchaikovsky, Foster, Chopin, Dvorak ("Going Home"). But then Lotte stripped off her gown, showing herself in tights. A thick rope came down from the ceiling—then, I hardly believe it now—I wouldn't have believed it if anyone had told me—Lotte climbed the rope like a sailor—carrying the violin—at the top she tucked one foot into a loop up there, thirty feet off the stage, and waved her bow. Russ began to yank the rope back and forth and, while Lotte swayed, she tucked the violin under her chin and played something from Puccini's *Madame Butterfly*.

There are times I imagined I had only dreamed that finale of Russ's act. I inquired of a nance, one of Russ's old loves, one night at Lipps, or the Flora, just what Russ was doing these days. "Oh, the old cow, he's gone to New York with that revolting creature. With their act. No, I haven't seen it. Really, *why* should I?"

I haven't heard of Russ or the act since.

Expatriates in Limbo

American expatriates in Paris usually knew each other, and borrowed from each other, made sex for each other, and lied a lot about each other. I was never too much interested in the writing crowd, or the painting set. Most of them talked a lot and carried dog-eared dirty manuscripts and hoped to be printed in *transition* (small *t*, please), or they smelled of turpentine and dirty feet and said Picasso was old hat, and anyway a fake.

I could mention two hundred Americans by name in Paris, and you never have heard of them. Oh, there were those who, like Robert McAlmon, Djuna Barnes, Elliot Paul, Man Ray, Natalie Barney, and Sylvia Beach, sometimes are mentioned today. But in the main, Americans in "the city of light" came to stay because it was cheap to live. Paris is beautiful, or they were buggers and clit bumpers, drunks, daffy seers like Raymond Duncan and lots of moochers.

Of course there were Gertrude and Ernest and Scotty and Ezra (after a while you didn't need last names, and it was class to use only their first names). But their egos gave me a pain in the ass. The only thing special about a good artist, is his work. And I've become tired of people asking me about them. We met and we talked at times, but they knew, and I knew, I wasn't looking for the one perfect word, or an avant-garde style of color slinging. I wasn't even going to try. I wasn't a writer, a deep thinker, and I wasn't a painter. I didn't compose like Virgil Thomson, or George Antheil who used airplane propellers in his *Ballet Mecanique*. I hung out with ex-soldiers, gamblers, horse-track people and speculators, loafers, sports in town for a tear. Paris is the key word. Paris, that's all.

You ate well, the girls were mostly willing. It was good to sit on a café terrace and know there wasn't a damn thing to do in the way of work. You lost the idea, if you were lucky, that Americans had a mission in the world, and you were guilty if you didn't have a goal. Guilty of what?

So Harry's New York Bar in Paris is the birthplace of the Bloody Mary and sidecar cocktail. Odd cocktails were dreamed up by the hundreds. Harry's folk used to ask for "sank roo doe noo," the bar address at 5 Rue Daunou.

Harry McElhone opened Thanksgiving Day in 1911. Harry McElhone was a Scots bartender with an eye on money. The mahogany bar warm to the touch of writers (name *any* dozen).

Harry's Bar was a damn easy place to be mooched on by shabby sentimental drunks, get picked up by an Irish chippy who claimed to be a duchess, and there was always a tout with nicotine-stained fingers who had a sure-thing horse running that day if you'd put nine hundred francs on it for both of you. The drinks were good at Harry's. And one of the editors on the *Herald* used to quote—some deep thinker—as he drank a raw egg in some brown sauce for his hangover…"I believe in the possibility of happiness if one…outlives the grosser passions, including optimism…Don't let the flesh be without sun, else spirit had no fight to win…"

Good as Harry's drinks were, he'd add, "Not up to the standard of the old Waldorf in New York or the Palace in San Francisco. College boys overcrowded the place." Also, he added, "Virgins from Vassar full of hope, and department-store buyers with douche bags among their trappings under their arm." Also nice Sinclair Lewis types sighing with delight and still not sure this was really Paris and a famous bar. Harry's.

You could get there tacky-eyed about noon in limping reluctance with your tongue hanging out, and the king of all hangovers hammering nails into your head. Chips and Bob, the two barmen, were ready for you. You'd get a sizzling fizzing aid or a glass of bicarb with a raw egg in it and some Worcestershire sauce to settle the coals still smoldering in your gut, and the hair of the dog in the shape of a neat shot glass full of brandy. Or three fingers of Dutch gin, unless you had incipient ulcers.

There would be a few other survivors of the night before standing around with mesmerized eyeballs, looking at the bottles or at the back of the bar, shaking their heads in a lazy way or just looking into their drinks as if the whole fucked-up answer to life were printed there. Somebody would be giving advice to a husband or a fag, plus sage que les sages. Or a crazy character in baggy dirty tweeds would be talking about his publisher or his broad. If you ate any lunch around two o'clock, you'd be leaning on the bar, or your ass screwed in a chair, and the place would fill up around you. Newspaper bums from the Paris *Herald*; the publisher-editor-owner of the English-language magazine, *Boulevardier*, a fellow named Erskine Gwynne, who was rumored to be a Vanderbilt; Elliot Paul, who was one of the editors of the avant-garde crock of crap *transition*, was a fat little butterball of a man—a pussy hunter with a goat's beard and lots of lies about his life in the Wild West, but with a poignant satanic joy, a proper feeder too, cooking up fine messes when in the mood, for American girl art students at Parsons that he'd invite up to sip and sample. Erskine and Elliot usually had been to a party the night before, and mostly they'd compare the women, the conversation, and the games played. I remember the morning I stood against the bar, holding on and waiting for the earth to steady itself, and Erskine and Elliot were at it.

"Sure were swacked, Paul."

"Not at all. Just the normal load on."

"You cheated on the game."

"Not at all."

"The most revolting whore in Paris for the prize, right?"

"And to bring the cunt back to the party, to be judged."

Paul laughed, his whole jellylike body shaking, "It was easy."

"Bullshit." Erskine turned to me, "Tell this bastard he cheated."

I didn't have much interest that morning in the games Americans played in Paris. "How did he cheat?"

"The sonofabitch. You see all the men had to go out, in half an hour come back with the most revolting whore in Paris, one still on her feet and walking the paves. You follow?"

"I follow."

"I bring back this old biddy who looked like a hag out of Brueghel, that painter chap, you know. All wrinkles, three teeth, all gums, a face Lautrec—why he'd have given his balls just to sketch her—broken nose, only three teeth, all pure Camembert...and Paul, the sonofabitch, his whore was declared the winner."

I said, "Don't tell me."

"She was no leper or anything," said Paul. "Fine relic, I'll admit. And as E. G.'s courtesan was about to be crowned, I lifted the skirt of my beauty and I had the winning ticket."

"The sonofabitch, you know why? His whore had one with-ered leg, the other was cork with metal joints, must have stolen it off a soldier of the war."

Paul smiled. "La belle dame sans merci."

"Very unfair, I mean when you bring a whore in parts. I bet her snatch was an old mop."

If it was a horse-race day, Harry's Bar would empty out, but around five, six, it would fill up, winners and losers, noses sunburned, and just plain drinkers. Some tourists would mosey in to look over the crowd. Often it would be second-class stuff; Kiki de Montparnasse, the gash of everybody, telling when she was a model how some artist would find her seated at the bar and kick out the stool from under her feet to see her fall on her marvelous ass. Or the Yid publisher from New York, who was trying to be one of the boys and was politely referred to as Mr. Shit. Sometimes Hemingway (he made a point of not liking to be called Ernest), playing the big manly stud, would come by; creeps from college with copies of Joyce in the blue paper covers from Sylvia's place, hoping Joyce would drop in and sign their copies. I guess it was at Harry's the story started of Jimmy Joyce standing at the bar and some college boy asking him, "Will you have a small whiskey on me, Mr. Joyce?" The answer, "There is no such thing as a small whiskey for an Irishman." I don't know if it happened like that or happened at all. Around midnight Roy Barton and Bud Sheppard would make music, piano and guitar.

Harry's was not a good place for the quiff hunters. For that there was the lobby of the Ritz for flappers and pubescent girls, or some of the cafés where the society tarts showed their legs and crotch, sitting back in a chair, toying with a rotten drink with lots of color in it. And Cocteau hunting boys, August John anything.

The real racing crowd went to the Chatham on the Rue Daunou, but lots of bets on the Grand Prix de Paris touted by "Peter Pickem" in the Chi *Trib* were made at Harry's, and some money changed hands. There would be a rolling of dice to see who paid for the drinks. Some drinkers stayed right through the dinner hour, just held up a finger and pointed to their empty glass. Some just stood or sat like statues of poured cement—the same color, too. But around nine, ten, women—hipless, titless, emaciated from reading *Vogue*—and their dates would come in, and there would be lots of laughing and making signals, canting altercations, and giving each other the office, arms around shoulders. Christ! The copious felicity, the involved malignity, and everybody drinking, laughing, scratching.

The serious drinkers didn't want to go anyplace, and the studs were comparing notes where the best parties were—alpha people, top drawer—and who would be there and what girl you could shaft, and what girl might, and what drip to avoid. Sherwood Anderson would tell some big story of how to get a virgin trapped and how to talk to her to give in and how to avoid tears. Sometimes a bull dyke on her way to Natalie's would bring in a flower dyke who wanted to meet Hendrik Van Loon, or a writer on the *Herald*. But mainly the lezs—they liked to call themselves Amazons—had their own little bars where they picked up clitoris-bumpers and sent each other tight little bunches of violets.

It was never as wild or as exciting as people said it was. But Harry's Bar was a place you could be wry and pungent, meet people you knew and people you wanted not to know. It had the smell and flavor of where you had come from. Nobody had any idea of going home if they could avoid it while little checks kept coming from home, or publishers, or a female friend. Checks from America were fine to have because the rate of exchange was very much in your favor, and you didn't have to take some old dame down to Monte or to Deauville as her joy-boy for coffee and cakes, a little champagne, a wrist watch, or a wop roadster.

The truth was, Harry's was an excuse lots of times for the writers not to write much when the Underwood was busted, and for the painters not to paint when the light was always bad.

The poets said they were meditating and incubating, and "you can't hurry a poem."

If you were in the chips and went to dances at the American Embassy, you bought your clothes at Old England on the Boulevard des Capucines; if not, you rummaged in the steamer trunk of someone still trusting and exciting who had come over on the *France*. It was never dull. You took a girl to the Sarah-Bernhardt to see Pierre Fresnay, the two Guitrys in *Mariette*, or the jazz band at the Jockey. Love began with an evening of hors d'oeuvres, ended in casual conviviality.

While waiting for funds if I had been gambling and losing, a date was taken to Clara Bow at the Paramount in *Wings*, and the Grand Guignol on the Rue Chaptal. And avoiding people you owed money to—the damned landlord, the hotel, all that got snotty shoving their addition in your face. Du sublime au ridicule il n'y a qu'un pas.

One month after some crazy play at cards and time with a greedy Hungarian whore, I was down to eating at parties given by Otto Kahn, or drinking at the showing off of a new statue in Joe Davidson's studio. Or even to being present at one of those dismal affairs Elsa Maxwell does for some rich old broad trying to make it in Paris society. With too much fastidiousness and sensibility you could starve in Paris. But I never got down to work as some Americans did at steering customers to Zelli's or the Scheherazade for a bit of a payoff. Once I lived off the sale of a Van Dongen drawing of a long-legged flapper for two weeks, eating the American cooking at Elza Lee's—the manager bought the drawing. Margaret Brown's was the other place that served American food; but you couldn't put it on the slate there; they never took a drawing or a small picture in pay. I had some credit in the Pigalle bars. I usually preferred Luigi's for lunch, but they didn't put your account on the slate either, cold cash only.

You can see it *was* name-dropping. For you not to be known by name was like being a nigger in Alabama. Even the bums and moochers had names the tourists knew. At least the tourists who were literary or artistic. I used to wear a beret when broke and not shave and they'd stand me drinks and ask, "How's the work going?"

Actually I liked Jimmy's Falstaff Bar better than Harry's. Jimmy had been a boxer from Liverpool, had worked at the Dingo. He was a confidante of the bar flies, and Jimmy liked best, as he put it, the hangers-on, the disillusioned (mainly as a result of love complications) and habitual drunks. Ernest took a lot of atmosphere and people from Jimmy's for *The Sun Also Rises*. Pat Guthrie and Duff Twysden, soaks who became Brett and Mike. Robert Cohn, the boxer who fell for Brett, was Harold Loeb, who nursed a small literary magazine that didn't last. Ernest was a Jew-baiter—maybe it didn't help his bias when Cohn copped Duff for a while. No, it wasn't a true picture; it was a good artist's legend.

I'm not going to put on my horn-rimmed glasses and do the literary bit here, or set down too much about the writing crowd in Paris. I wasn't part of their ménages, even if I knew them pretty well. Everybody I figure is going to dissect them; the professors and the survivors. But Ernest, a bastard with his friends and his women, his games of sport, drink, food, was playing with himself. He was a sixteen-jewel genius when Gertrude and maybe Sherwood Anderson showed him he was writing wrong and they could show him how to make it hit close to physical skin-to-skin contact. Those early stories have the rasp and the touch of the real thing, of the real things that mattered to him. Maybe Ernest couldn't think, and his characters can only taste whiskey and dream of unreal fucking out of myths, and make a romance out of killing animals and fish, and dying. Shit, death is God's vulgar, dirty, painful trick, and anyone could have dreamed up a better way of doing things. But give Ernest his due. He had genius once.

The way I see it, the American expatriates were kidding themselves. They thought they were hard nuts, realists. Naturalists like Zola only with more class, a little James Joyce—Freud-sauce added. It was the idea of being special and classy that kept them from seeing things right. They were bloody romantics; we all know that crap about "the lost generation" and Scott's "all the sad young men." Few really knew life down in the dirt, a lousy job and a noisy family. They used the Great War, which some only touched, driving ambulances or sending out press items— they felt the war had made them hard and real. It just made them blind. They had hurt their finger and wanted the world to kiss it—like Mommy. They were all goddamn puritans, even if pansies or dykes or communists, or avoiding meat, eating hay. They fed off each other—not life.

That's what's wrong with Jay Gatsby. Scott never knew a real killer, a gang lord, a mean hard-nosed bootlegger, which Gatsby was supposed to be. A big-shot rackets man. If he were, he'd not have shown Daisy silk shirts, he'd have fucked the ass off of her and pistol-whipped Tom, her husband, and ended up running New York City. Romantics don't become Al Capones, nor do real Gatsbys yearn over a lost love. It's still a fine book, but it's a dream of a lace-curtain Irish poor kid snob, writing about scoring with the quality.

Paris failed them all in time—it only waxed their romantic surfaces. I saw their fat fun turned thin; they killed themselves, or became rummies, or went home to run the Ford Agency in Busted Balls, Idaho, if they could pass their Wassermans. I wasn't much better, but I didn't hang a sign around my neck: ARTIST— VERY SENSITIVE.

The Skin Trade

The romantic tone of Americans in Paris showed in their idea about sex.

Skipping the impotent and the pederasts, all the nookie hunters among the Americans had their heads filled with pictures of sleek Parisian tarts and hustlers, images already out of date, and mixed up with sepia-colored photos of 69 and muff-diving sold to them as "French postal cards." After a while most, if they didn't have a steady lay among the US art students, or weren't too hot for the fancy parties given by the Porters or the visitors at the Ritz, would drift down to the Boulevard Edgar-Quinet or the Rue de Fourcy, sip a bock and enjoy the life, sleazy and busy in the brasseries, kid a couple of whores and buy some drinks, swallow cacahuètes (peanuts), but not hurry into anything. There might be some of the big pink Normandy hookers at the Chope du Nègre. Mostly it was the Rue du Faubourg Montmartre when our friends were looking for something in the skin trade and weren't flush enough to afford something no better but fancier, in silk and furs.

The college boys with their letters of introduction or frat brothers I'd take down the line would all go bug-eyed and kind of grin and tell me they felt, oh hell, "No puritan guilt here." No need to act up at all, I'd say, even if there were maquereaux and souteneurs, the streetwalkers' pimps, smoking their foul cigarette butts and paring their finger-nails with a sharp frog-sticker. I'd walk the boys over to the Halles and get them the expected onion soup and let them look over the parading cunt. Filling them full of oysters and clams at the Chien qui Fume, telling them it would put lead in their pencils, I found a lot of them were still cherry. Some would act shy, if they were just in town a week or so, their Hart, Schaffner and Marx still well pressed, and so I'd have some of the tarts come on over and jolly the boys a bit and rub their hips against a Yale man or a blushing kid from Princeton, and say "O, le pauvre bébé!"

Paris whores have a nice sense of camaraderie, but also they are all business—no heart-of-gold types, the kind American writers from the Middle West like to put in their novels. Hell, these hustlers were mostly wily small-town girls who had come to Paris to peddle their ass and get enough of a bank account together for a dowry so they could marry some clod-kicker back home, or make a down payment on a bar and eating place, and be so goddamn respectable the rest of their lives you couldn't even pinch a tit while paying your bill. Or they died in one of those big dirty hospitals, asking the sister for a priest.

The college boys would buy the whores white wine, a Pernod, café crème, crème de menthe au cassis, or a shot of apple brandy on a rainy night. The tarts were hungry, but I don't know why it was that sandwiches, a brioche, an omelette would take the romance out of it for the boys. They bought drinks, but it seemed to spoil a whore with sore feet and tired eyes for them that she could be hungry.

I explained to the college boys a good whore was sérieuse about her work and game for anything. A whore who wasn't earnest was a tramp, a boozer, a drug sniffer, or daffy from chewing hashish which the Arab rug peddlers sold them. A good whore, Sherwood Anderson had said, "knows she is sitting on three square meals a day."

After a while the boys would wander off with one of the tarts to a cheap hotel, the girl hanging on tight, dark silk shiny on big rumps, pretty breasts sometimes bobbing out of the top of her blouse, the tart talking salty street French to some kid from Cornell or Stanford whose two-year college course of the language failed him, and he perhaps wondering how he'd perform in the hot-sheet hotel. And would he get the clap and did the maquereau really not mind selling his girl?

It was very American, thinking of this kind, worrying if a pimp minded selling his girl's body. Also if some souteneur began to slap his woman around in a bar, hard blows back and forth across her cheeks with the palm and back of his hand, I had to explain that the girl expected it, was sure her pimp was showing his love by giving her punishment: "He cared." It's hard for Americans to understand that some lower-middle-class women expect to be beaten by a lover.

"That's too low," a college boy said.

Sure, still I knew some high-class American flappers who didn't mind a chop to the chin before getting into bed.

It was pretty shocking to lots of Americans. In their culture, hitting a woman is not a traditional sign of full possession. If they were shy Americans, not at ease in cafés or under street lights picking up a whore, settling the business of price and place, I'd suggest to them to go to the whorehouses, or "closed houses"— the French term. Running a cathouse in Paris is almost a family heritage, and respectable—as respectable as auto repairing or pol-

itics anyway. A good house, polite, established with old customers and a family trade, say fathers and sons and sons-in-law, was
as respectable and ordinary as a greengrocer's. A good closed
house had no drunks rolling on the dusty rugs, and your wallet
was safe along with your inherited grandfather's gold watch and
chain. The girls would not reach for your whang right away or
tell you dirty stories, or get boozed up and scream and carry on.

It was a serious parlor; oil lamps or gas fixtures converted
to electric light, wax flowers under glass, girls and clients sitting
around like on a pleasant minor holiday or saint's day. Sometimes a man would even bring his wife to show her what life
was like in a cozy maison de tolérance; of course saying he had
heard much of such places, though he didn't himself go there,
but his friends, his boss liked to faire l'amant. The Madame would
grin, he most likely being a cocksman and known to every girl
in the place as a stud stallion.

Ernest and Scotty liked to get their fun by bringing people
to the more lively places, but neither of them was what could
be called a real gash-hound. They hung sex all over with romantic trimmings.

American writers—mostly lousy lays, the chippies told me—
didn't like the respectable family places. They went to the tableaux
vivants, joints that had circus acts, sex fantasy acted out for real.
Where the women and men perform by copping joints, the women
picking up coins with their snatches. Going up Hersey Road,
you'd see good decent Americans shiver with awe and a fine
delight in sin at all this. Performers dressed as admirals buggering sailors, sailors diving on nuns, and a nun being had by Shet-
land ponies or sheep dogs. The Rue de la Victoire was the place
for these shows. At some joints I remember seeing Wall Street
Bankers, Meadowbrook polo players, a Pulitzer Prize winner. Most
popular were the Sphinx and the Chabannais, almost continual
circuses. One of the regular boys taking on an "admiral" in such
a lineup later became a very famous and very fine French film

actor. As he explained it to me a long time later, with a shrug, "It was a trade, and I was hungry and very poor. The quartier was poor, we all were poor. It was eating and drinking. The night I stopped all that was when in my sailor suit I looked around and there was an uncle of mine, done up as an admiral—the sod—climbing up my arse."

Unlike most sporting houses in the USA catering to the passing scene, the steady clientele of a closed house was very loyal to it, and you didn't even have to open your fly. You'd drink a brandy, read the *Paris Soir*, listen to some music, greet other customers resting their pratt on the leather sofas or cozy around a table, smoking and making small Frenchy jokes, mostly about priests and water closets, or General Joffre's cock.

What gave it away as a snatch shop was the girls were mostly naked, or just wearing stockings and high-heeled slippers, a bit of lace, and they were singing, "J'aime à jamais." In winter the stove would be overcooking the air, and in summer there would be little buzzing brass electric fans with tricolored ribbons tied to the frames, and the ice in the drinks—if there was ice—would taste like Typhoid Mary.

Closed houses were mostly too bourgeois for those from the USA escaping American morality, and they would go find the alcoholics, foul-mouthed whores who were not at all sérieuse. Sometimes we'd have to go to Harry's or Jimmy's bar, to see if we could get some American out of jail if he had run into trouble with the law. The French flics would usually have worked them over just a bit—not hard as they did the French. The Paris cop is a big mean shit at all times, comes mostly from Corsica, and smells of rum and garlic.

It was Elliot Paul who put it all in its proper place one night, while the gérant of a respectable family whorehouse was serving us coffee. "What most Americans object to in a family business like this, Madame and Monsieur Whoremaster, six plump girls, all going to mass and confession, and cousins of Madame, is that there is no sense of sin, no guilty voluptuousness goes with it. Too open and casual; so easy just saying 'Je suis prêt.' But make it a place where your American Babbit or adolescent has to sneak into, and where it's against the law, and you strip in the dark and the broad is shy about getting your joint copped, and an abandonment of principles is a sure one-way ticket to hellfire and the devil's pitchfork, whoopee! Your American will be having the time of his life."

I ordered les alcools all round.

The closed house has the smell of spilled drink and dreadful French tobacco, body powder and sweat, and a hint of cooking with herbs, and often there's an old aunt as housekeeper, once a courtesan or can-can dancer, or retired from a maison de couture. The decor is lovely—all the crap of six generations; some dead relative in oil paint on the wall, draped in black; sea shells from holidays in August by Madame and Monsieur in the south of France; Monsieur in tropical soldier's gear in Indochina, fat and pink like a roasting pig.

There were also dives where American women could find Amazons to their taste, or Natalie Barney would invite them over for some lesbian revels. The sissies could find trade in tight pants with a golden head of curls in the Cocteau set or the fairy writers who adored Gertrude Stein. It was surprising the fancy or important-named Americans in business and politics who went faggot in Paris. The arts, the music schools were just loaded with USA talent, if not genius, composing and admiring the behinds of the waiters and the greedy school boys offering themselves. That was the way Paris had been and was, and the way it would always be for the fun-loving Americans; the place where you can trade your dreams for something solid.

Aleister Crowley and Company

Much more interesting than most of the howlers and movers at 27 Rue de Fleurus, among the colonies of Americans and English in Paris, was Aleister Crowley. I had introduced Ernest to him, but Ernest was always a bit wary of those things outside his range. Gertrude had called E. H. yellow. I knew what she meant. Other Americans over their aperitifs, found Crowley fascinating but a bit sinister to get too close to. In the 1920s, Crowley himself was a bit on the fat side, not too clean looking, bald, giving the impression of a poorly modeled statue of the Buddha that had been through a bad ceramic firing. I have seen him sniff cocaine as if it were a fresh sea breeze. It was a very fashionable for some time among groups, closely watched by the agents de police, to sniff "snow," as some called it, and the addicts were called snowbirds among the Americans.

I wasn't a Crowley cult follower nor had much interest in his Black Mass sessions, mostly sexual exhibitionism with the rites of Holy Rome burlesqued. For me, sex was never a spectator sport—if I can't play, I don't much care to watch.

Aleister Crowley was a mystic, a cabalist, semi-leaner on Blavatsky's Theosophical Society, with the added charm of a drug addict, sensualist, "pervert," poet, seer, and producer of an irreverent ritual Mass in Paris for paying guests, Americans among them. The goat used to deflower the virgin was real; the virgin one had to take on pure faith.

Crowley tried to explain to me his Law of Thelma and the cult of Ordo Templi Orientis—mostly, I sensed, it was all dedicated to drugs, torture, and sexual orgies. "I don't give a damn for the whole human race—you're nothing but a pack of cards. I admire the Roman Emperor who wished all the world had one neck so he could cut it off." What appealed to some of his American converts, mostly women who slashed their bodies with knives in certain nasty rituals, was the basic Law of Thelma: "There is no law beyond Do what thou wilt...Do what thou wilt shall be the whole of the Law."

In a Paris, where it was hard to shock, Crowley shocked. With his scarred mistresses and his sacred prostitutes. He was a gourmet who drank Napoleon brandy (or what is called by that name). Opium, cocaine, hashish he used from time to time. Arabs sold the drugs in Paris, often acting as rug peddlers.

Was he really evil? Sinister sure, maybe dangerous as the Demon Chorozon—but funny too...saying, "I have crossed the Abyss beyond good and evil."

There was no one of his power and madness ruling any other nasty fun cult in Paris. The other diabolic manifestation among the American salons was kid's stuff. Scatological vice maybe—some warping of the American puritanical past. *Do what thou wilt*—sure—but mostly within reason. "After all, one needed eight hours sleep a night."

Some Americans were Crowley's special victims or dupes. During the World War he went to the United States, wrote for pro-German publications. A girl I knew in New York told me of Leah Faesi, a singing teacher who became his Scarlet Woman, moved into his Greenwich Village apartment. He painted her nude as *A Dead Soul*, consecrated her "a companion of the Beast," branded her on the breasts. Leah used to sit around his apartment naked, an incarnation of the goddesses Astarte and Isis. When later I lived in the Village, I found they still remembered him and her.

The press wrote of his orgies; couples danced about, twirling to wild music, reciting obscene verse, girls undressing, cutting themselves on the tits. It all—all but the knife work—seemed like certain Sundays in Paris.

Crowley, while playing the Passion Pope, gave off a sweet, nauseous odor, his Perfume of Immortality; a sex-appeal ointment, and he said it gave him power, particularly over women, and on the boulevards horses whinnied at him. He also took doses of laudanum, veronal, and anhalonium as a one-man drug epidemic and sign painter. He loved his slogans—EVERY MAN AND WOMAN IS A STAR. DO WHAT THOU WILT SHALL BE THE WHOLE OF THE LAW.

Some of his American converts had strange name changes. A man from Bridgeport, Connecticut, Samuel A. Jacob, became SHMUEL Bar AIWAZ bie YACKOU de SHERABAD, incarnating the Lost Word of Freemasonry, with the value 418, "the number of the Magical Formula of the Aeon." The Grand Treasurer of the Ordo Templi. Orientis was a deaf-mute, George Cowie, VIII, Frater Fiat, Pax., etc., etc. He and the Grand Secretary ran off with the Order's money while Crowley was initiating a Sister Cypris into the Truth of Passions. H. L. Mencken was introduced to the Ape of Thoth, she all in a black suit with the silver and scarlet Star of the Temple. But *this* H. L. Mencken, Crowley told me, turned out to be a businessman of the same name as the Baltimore boob-buster.

Crowley saw himself as a sexual genius above the normal hardon master—yet with breasts that suggest a sort of hermaphrodite.

Crowley certainly gave Paris an added excitement. Pain was part of the thrill he gave women. Many were drunks, hysterics. One who showed disbelief he punished in his own way. "I have unusually pointed canine teeth. I fix a fold of flesh between the two points; and then, beating time with one hand, suddenly snap, thus leaving two neat indentations on the flesh concerned." An orgy followed...twelve hours of "insane intoxication."

From 1920 on, he shocked Europe, established his abbey as the Temple of Thelmic Mysteries. He explained to me its magic circles and pentagrams, red-tiled floor, a six-sided altar opposite the Throne of the Beast, a burning brazier and ritual dagger, the Throne of the Scarlet Woman nearby. I saw some of Crowley's paintings of the sexual acts, fuckings, in every conceivable position. Good, but he was no Matisse.

I never attended the full rites he described—he was afraid I'd laugh at the wrong time. He wrote in some book he gave me, "My house...the whore's hell, a secret place of the quenchless fires of Lust and the eternal torment of Love." He believed in two concubines at a time, and his rites of love were noisy, one of the girls told me; sex à trois, the ceremonies "wild to the point of insanity."

He used to officiate at these sexual-religious rites as experiences of magical affirmation done to hymns, prayers, and symbolic acts to achieve high states of consciousness. He fed the followers the Cakes of Light to bring on lust. One gossiped of sexual intercourse between a goat and the Scarlet Woman, the blood of a cock, symbol of concupiscence, gulped as a sacrifice.

After I had left Paris, he was kicked out of France; a Paris paper wrote he was a German secret agent. Maybe he was. I used to stand him a brandy when I was flush, as I liked to hear him talk. I felt he was one of those cunt-struck men who had to invent outré games to explain what was just an itch, and a desire to hurt what they felt had a hold on them. That's why all the slashing and biting of female flesh, and the whipping and drugging. So perhaps he would have understood my grandfather's remark, "Cunt may be the most important thing in the world; too bad we have to go to a woman for it."

As for Crowley's concubines, I got to know rather well at the cost of most of my allowance, one of them, an artist's model called Trudy, an English girl with a dark little fox face whom I suspected of being Eurasian. "Filthy old goat he was—but what could I do? Models aren't in demand as much as they used to be. It's all that Picasso! Wine glasses and guitars, *that* stuff!"

Perhaps the female body was no longer needed as pattern or inspiration by the avant-garde—but most American painters in Paris had a favorite model. The artist's model had had a hundred years of fame and the café had been the models' headquarters. Pascin told me he had made a study of the history of models. He would. In Whistler's day he said it was the Brasserie des Martyrs, then moved to the Café Guerbois. Then Montmartre and the Lapin Agile of Picasso; the artists moved to the Dôme and the Rotonde in Montparnasse, the models followed. It was there Americans went to buy drinks for the blonde negress model, "Queen of the cubists," Aicha Goblet, a circus rider brought to Montparnasse by Pascin. Aicha cooked for the artists, lent money, and protected them from moochers. Utrillo's mother, Suzanne Valadon, had posed for Dégas, Renoir, and Lautrec, and was a hell of a fine painter. The true favorite of the Americans was Kiki. She was dark, splendidly built and gay, very available. Kiki's straight bangs, long nose and odd clothes made her a Paris character. Kiki was the daughter of a Frenchwoman named Prins. She told Americans she sold flowers on the streets at fourteen, was later a drudge in a butcher's house, a bookseller, and bottle washer. She was the favorite model of Japanese painter Tsugouharu Foujita, posed for Moise Kisling, Kees van Dongen, Man Ray, others. Love and drink did damage her. She was particularly fond of young Americans. I'd listen to them tell of their adventures with her in sex in Paris. "She was never able to grow pubic hair, you know." Hardly the study their folks had sent them to Paris for.

I have one memento of Aleister Crowley. I wrote down what he thought of organized religion—*other* religions of course: "After the prophet, comes the disciples and the myths, after the disciples comes the church and the miracles, and with the church comes the betrayal of the prophet and the growth of the hierarchy..."

Also in Paris there is always at least once a week an American who thinks he knows you—grabs you in Jimmy's or Harry's or the lobby of the George V. I made a note of a usual conversation in a bar, a monologue one morning by a large, fast-talking, hand-shaking gent:

"Hello, hello. I'm Harry L——. You know my brother George, the lawyer. I'll tell him I saw you in Paris. Joe and me, we bought up the K—— New Jersey food markets. That's right...Him. Joe's wife died, you know. Last year, suddenly. A picture of health one day, the next—well... What? You think I look like George? People say that. Wanted to come to Paris, go to the music school. I said, Georgie, be a lawyer, lawyers do good. Don't louse up your life playing a fiddle. Married Gussie K——, of the Troy, New York people. Lumber. Matt's in Paris, the whole family. Made a pile converting Maryland farm lands to cottages—Cape Codders. Had a deal with him on some acres outside Palm Beach—that's the boom place again soon. Surf-glow Estates. Got this friend—in gems, diamonds, lives on Surf Road up that way. Zuggie M——. Your Uncle A—— knows Zuggie. We did a lot of apartment houses packaging, fifteen, twenty years ago. Smart, that Zuggie. Those days didn't have one dime to rub against another dime he could spare. Five daughters. Yet when each one was married, bought 'em a house, put a big mortgage on each house. Today, *ho ho*—Zuggie, give or take, he's worth in the millions. And he held on to the Palm Beach stuff—quality acres."

Damn if I remembered him. My Uncle A—— was a sporting uncle who won and lost silver mines in Leadville in the old days with Horace Tabor.

No matter where the Americans came from, you could usually sell them a volume of Joyce. Most were not literary, but had heard it was a "dirty" book. You had to split with a reporter on the *Herald* who could do the James Joyce signature with a real feel, and even add a personal message. Of course Joyce, if you caught him before he got plastered on white wine, he'd be happy to sign one of the blue-covered books. He sang too, but I couldn't make any money on that.

A Bohemian Almanac

Inside Greenwich Village

After my first three years in Paris, I came back to America for a spell—that is, I got to New York. Which is not like the rest of America, but with a flavor all its own. It was a wilder New York—spinning in a different pattern than when I had last seen it as a seventeen-year-old kid catching a train at Grand Central for Canada. You were not supposed to like New York. The Paris crowd all said it was crass and commercial, materialistic, greedy, and ruled by rum runners and bootleggers. I have to confess I rather liked the city in the mid-twenties. At least from the Village where I settled in to wait for the family lawyers, those Daumier sharks' heads in their Wall Street offices milking family trusts, to allow me more money. My grandfather had at last shuffled out of life, drinking bad Scotch and reading Mary Baker Eddy. The last letter I had from him, answering mine asking him for enough money to live in Paris, contained a line I never forgot, written with his broad-nib Waterman fountain pen: "In this world a man has to stick his thumb up his ass, then lift himself off the ground and take stock of himself." I never tried it, but I understood the message: not a dime in his will to me personally. His money and stocks went into a foundation of endowed loafers from various colleges.

While waiting for some kind of word from the trust lawyers, I had my English and French dentistry gone over by Doc Eli G——.

"Gevalt! The momsers who did *this*, repaired steam rollers."

A marvelous Jewish artist who set me up with gold inlays and did some prolonged root canal work; gave me a smile such as maybe the Mona Lisa would have had, had she opened her mouth. Eli, the dentist, was a high liver. "All us Yiddles are either pious tailors or bon vivants." Eli wore two-toned shoes and took me to Minsky's. He kept a high-yellow girl named Lily in Harlem. "At home I have a Jewish princess in the Bronx, with three rotten sassy kids and a castrating mother. She wears my father's balls hanging from her ears; people think they are pearls. She can't cook a tzimmes, hates kids, is skinny like a pencil. What kind of Jewish mother is that?"

Eli wanted to pilot a plane, fly in the worst way, and that is how he did fly—with no sense of balance, no feel for the stick. He owned an old DH4 biplane. It had been designed in England as a bomber, but built in the United States. These ships had been tried as carriers of the first US Air Mail, and had killed a lot of pilots, and you could pick one up cheap; they were sturdy. Eli had his plane out on a field near Jamaica, Long Island. I took him up at least twice a week. In two months he was going solo; not a splendid flyer, but with style. He was going to fly us that fall—me, him, and Lily the yellow girl, to Miami and go after sailfish and real estate. Eli took the crate up at dusk—alone—two days before the start of our trip. He took off fine and flew very steady. Coming in from the other end of the field, no one had bothered to tell him a new temporary power line had been strung up. He hit it, and that was the end of the DH4 and Eli with a 150 h.p. engine sitting on him, and a fire that practically did a professional cremation job.

The estate billed me for the dentistry work I was to get free for the flying lessons. The Jewish princess, his wife, mother, and a brother-in-law, started a story that it wasn't Eli at all in the plane all burned up. But just some Bowery bum we had gotten into the plane, and that Eli was in Brazil living it up with Lily, the high-yellow. I liked that story. But of course in real life there is no tight plot like that. A fellow dentist identified Eli's teeth, and after a while the lawyer's letters stopped coming demanding payment from me.

I felt safer in the Village with only degenerates, drunks, sex maniacs, geniuses, professional arsonists, abortionists, and fakes, rather than in uptown New York. The trouble with Jews, Lily used to explain to me, is that they are too moral and feel they have an order to keep the world God-loving and kind, and place family life in the center of the universe. Poor Eli never had a chance, Lily said, "With all that goodness, and ass-wiping mother love, a castrated father and a don't-touch-me wife and them three smart children who got all As and Bs. Sheet!"

I had to agree. People don't like decency pointed out to them as examples to follow. Poor Eli. I remember him drinking his hooch and sighing, "What kind of husband am I? I never have knocked down my wife, batted her in the mush."

Everybody, after the war, was telling me the Village wasn't what it had been. I heard how it had been when the arty crowd of before the war—Carl Van Vechten and others—found it "creative"—a word I connect with fancy talk and bad breath. I had a letter of hello to Carl from Gertrude Stein, and I could see very soon, watching him shake down his ruby cuff links, he wasn't my kind. I didn't give a damn about high art or causes.

And after having some stinking hooch with him and Robert Edmund Jones, me telling them about Isadora Duncan's problems, I went down to Washington Square South and found myself a room near Romany Marie's tearoom. I waited for my uncle's lawyers to get some money from a family trust, so I could get back to Paris. Then and later, I horsed around with a fine girl named Olga I met through "Jimmie" Criswall (Eliza Helen Criswall), who ran the Mad Hatter for some time. I was getting to know the Village—going from a speakeasy to a tearoom to some club meeting. I got to say hello to the same faces, and I'd chivy the changing uptown crowd come to look at the freaks. The girl Olga liked joints; the Crumperie and the Vermillion Hound, the Polly-woggie, the Kricket, Steps Down, the Jumble Shop (I'm guessing at the spellings). The natives are artistic talking—those that don't really paint or write—also the outsiders who come to grab off the best flats and studios—the natives didn't have much money. The Purple Pup called itself "Montmartre in New York—make it a habit not an OCCASION." It was as close to Montmartre as a pig's ass is to a lover's kiss.

Olga—I was living with her—painted lampshades on fake parchment, and I'd help her carry them to Wanamaker's and certain Madison Avenue shops where she took orders for shades picturing snow scenes and pirate ships and birds. She'd paint them in her one-room studio with a closet kitchen, and I'd color the backgrounds. When we figured we'd made enough for a night of it, we'd wash up, go find Bobby Edwards who ran a magazine, *The Quill*, or go to Jimmie's Mad Hatter and sit under the wall sign Olga had painted: WE'RE ALL MAD HERE...I'M MAD, YOU'RE MAD...YOU MUST BE OR YOU WOULDN'T BE HERE. And another sign advertising the proud boast that the joint provided CANDLELIGHT, COFFEE AND CONVER-SATION. On a bad night, you heard of a dozen busted love affairs, over fair coffee.

Jimmie was being courted by this fat Dutchman, Hendrik

Willem Van Loon, whom I had known in Paris—who practically
lived in the joint. Always talking up a hurricane. There wasn't
anything he didn't know about in detail, even if he was often
wrong, and he made miserable drawings on everything, even marking up the walls. I liked Willie because he was a real wrong guy;
a fake, Jimmie said, doing the culture bit. There was something
wrong in him about women. He'd make a play for a woman on
sight, and act like a kid with a new red wagon. Romany Marie
explained to Olga and me, "The Dutchie is a bag of wind, and
when I was born in a forest of Molsavia, my people knew how
to tell if a man was real."

Olga put a fresh cigarette in her long holder, "Come off it,
Marie. You were born in a pushcart shed on Delancy Street."

So there would start a slanging match between the two and
if we had sold enough lampshades, we went across Sixth Avenue
to Christopher Street Sheridan Square to Don Dickerman—he
ran this really Toyland night club, the Pirates' Den. All false pirate gear and sleazy wall decorations. The booze was as bad as
the music. A poet from Chicago, Max, would sometimes get tossed
out of the place for mooching the uptown trade. He'd stand on
the curb, his dong out, saying things like: "To piss in frontier
mood in the dead leaves of autumn." It was worth me buying
him a shot.

Olga was very much a mind type—ideas smoked in her head.
She was given to moving around among the intelligentsia of the
downtown brain types—painting scenery for little theatre groups
like the followers of the Provincetown Players. And there everyone talked about Gene, who turned out to be Eugene O'Neill,
a serious horse-faced young booze fighter. But not soft and weepy
like some drunks. Just full of ass-dragging dark thought; a sad
feeling that "life is a bucket of shit," to quote Gene. I got along
fine with him. I had his itch to drink, in fact at times I had it
bad, but I didn't have the problem Gene had; I could hold it
better and didn't get me down. We'd be bellying the bar in some

speak, or squatting in some dusty studio, and I remember him looking the true Black Mick he was, and saying things. One time: "Better not to be born. Better to have been nothing." But in a whisper that didn't carry.

I said, "Come off it, Gene. That's pretty easy poetry." He was well established as a playwright by then. Uptown was playing his dramas, but he liked to come down to the Village, being, I think, shy and all wrapped up in deep thinking about man's sad destiny; that's a load which didn't bother me. I liked Shakespeare's line about us eating a fish that didn't eat off a worm, that ate off a king. W. S. must have been a gourmet, and Gene wasn't.

"It is the only life we have," I told Olga, "and one had to live it out like an old suit." I said, "You can get so comfortable in it, you hate to throw it to some bum." Olga said I was a god-damn fucking Philistine and Gene was a genius. I said she didn't mind the effing part did she? So we shook dust out of the studio bed to prove it. I felt we'd stay clear of Gene for a while.

For all his success, I thought Gene's plays humorless and deadly bores. Except for the sailor things, the one-actors he did. The *Emperor Jones* was just a great big show-off part for an actor. I saw Paul Robeson play the hell out of it and it worked. *The Hairy Ape* and *Beyond the Horizon* I thought college-boy Gloomy-Gus stuff, but the downtown and uptown ate it. I think he won a Pulitzer for one of them.

The character who had the Village figured just right was a Latvian, a little sawed-off fellow named Barney, who ran the Greenwich Village Inn. The college boys, stockbrokers, and ad copy writers could pick up girls from the *Greenwich Village Follies* or a show called *Hobohemia*. Barney got arrested for selling liquor after the Big Dry Up. Olga said arrest wasn't enough, "He should be shot, selling that stuff." Olga and I were doing a lot of drinking at the Inn; the stuff wasn't really fatal. Barney had done thirty days in the Tombs, claimed to be the first man sent to the cooler for selling liquor against the Volstead Act.

Soon everybody was making and selling wine and what passed for whiskey and gin, and New York kidneys proved to be heroes. Beer was needled with ether to make it give you a jolt. Truth was, it was not art or music or theatre or literature that brought people with fat wallets to the Village. It was to drink and get laid. That's the direct truth without any fancy excuse or Floyd Dell's moonshine prose. The Village girls were mostly willing and available. The Free Love, which wasn't that free, had Emma Goldman as its goddess. Emma was no beauty, "But had a beautiful soul," Olga said. She was also a marvelous cook. I once ate her potato lotkas and pot roast; a splendid gourmet was lost to some too serious talks of Ibsen, and cries of "to the barricades! and down with the capitalist pigs!" This was after she was run out of the new Russia by Soviet world savers. Do-gooders, I've noticed, want to reform you—not themselves.

There were real odd citizens, even for the Village. There was the Baroness crazy-crazy. The story was that she was the wife of a German baron, Von Freytag Von Loringhoven, a baron who left her in isolated high living, but high and dry at the Ritz when he went back to Germany for the war of 1914-18. Elsa was no beauty, being already middle-aged, thin, and showing lots of ungainly bone. She moved to the Village where living was reasonable as to cost, and worked in a cigarette factory. She also posed for some of the art students, but never lost that German nose-in-the-art, get-the-goddamn-peasants-out-of-my-way composure. Art Young, the *Masses* cartoonist, knew her well, and through him I met her. Someone had knocked out some of her front teeth, so she looked like a skull made into an ashtray, and someone else got her around to painting cubist oils, writing Dada poetry. Which is much the easiest kind to write, as Art said, "if your marbles are missing." She had three dogs in residence, and the place stank of her collection of turds. The costumes she wore were eccentric without having much style. At one time, she shaved off all her hair, painted her

Heinie skull with scarlet lacquer. I told her it improved her appearance.

She said, "Freheit ist nur dem reich der Traume." She was *real* Dada, not Duchamp's chic chichi; she wore postage stamps instead of rouge, and also used them for wallpaper. For a hat, she often wore a strawberry fruit basket. She fought cops every chance she got and took several rides to the can in the Black Maria, sitting in the paddy wagon as though it were a royal coach. The poor raddled bitch really had style.

She became notorious in the Village when the reporters began to buy her drinks, and lots of jokers used her for their ideas of fun. She was being invited to parties just to see how she would act up. It was, in its way, like baiting the bulls in Spain that got Ernest so hot in the groin.

Olga and I went to one party for some opera star and the singer went popeyed to see Baroness Else come in wearing a coal scuttle like a German trench helmet, with spoons, for a hat, and she had added some of her pink postage stamp cosmetics and yellow paint as skin tone. Her lips were done in black. Olga said, "Woodrow Wilson, six months dead."

The opera singer was a polite lady and she and the Baroness began to carry on a conversation. The singer, to point up her place in the world of art, insisted she sang "only for humanity."

Baroness Elsa's answer to that was, "I wouldn't lift my leg to piss like a dog for humanity."

The talk was in the Village that the Baroness couldn't pass a Wasserman, was riddled with the Old Rale. So the knowing lads gave her a wide berth in that department.

Later, on a return trip to New York from Europe, I decided my favorite nut was Joe Gould, a little bit of a man, an egg-bald head with a goatlike wisp of a beard. He told everyone he was writing an "Oral History of the World." He was always carrying a briefcase of papers and said it was the work in progress, like James Joyce's. It would run to millions of words, he assured us.

His real desire was to get loaded as quickly as he could on free drinks. Being under a hundred pounds and kind of shriveled up like a spider held in a candle flame, it didn't take much to get him going. But he could keep on knocking back the drinks as long as someone was buying. When good and sloshed, he would start running in a circle at a good pace, mouth open, little beard in the air, flapping his arms and trying to go *caw! caw!* like a seagull. The New York newspapers, always looking for queer characters to sweeten the drivel they presented as world shaking, began to call him "Professor Seagull." Some people took it up. Joe was supposed to live off the bread people tossed to the birds in Washington Square, but I think that was another newspaper lie.

Joe always saw himself as a dancer, and he'd throw himself around a cleared space any place, in what he called "the Joseph Ferdinand Gould Stomp." It wasn't very funny. Certainly not rewarding. For he existed in hallways, slept in subways. When in control of a few coins on a real cold night, he gave his trade to the Bedbug Waldorfs; the flophouses. I never found the misery of poverty very jolly—and to me Joe wasn't amusing. He was always supposed to be writing away at the thousands of words in his "Oral History of the World." I never saw him do any work, but that didn't matter, Barney said "A lot of the writers and painters in the Village don't appear to work much. Better so—you ever see what it is when they do?"

But there were those who did, and I got to hate the smell of turpentine as much as cat pee. Olga always found some new genius and gave his work houseroom. The reading of poetry was more of a pain in the ass. Poets run to tooth-rot and Limberger breath. So having some shaggy verse-maker spit out his stanzas gave me the willies. I didn't attend any too many of these sessions. Half were pansies, some flogged their meat in subways. I usually would wander off toward McSorley's Saloon, or what claimed to be the place, where you went in the back way and drank some dreadful beer.

There were a lot of addlepated show-offs downtown, and some were lovable and some were horrors. Folks said the place was a fake; everyone told me it was not what it had been in the great old days when real writers and painters were in the majority. There are thousands of painters and artists in Paris, but only a handful of the real red meat of genius, and a dozen or so being built up by galleries and critics I wouldn't trust a female dog with.

I always had the feeling James Joyce might have gone around with his packets of writing under his arm like Joe Gould, if some kind ladies hadn't stepped in and pushed him hard. He was a drunk too, like Joe—but you forgive a success. Jimmy Joyce was a marvelous Celtic con man and a genius. Joe Gould should have taken lessons from him.

Life with Olga

To put down a Villager, you just had to say it wasn't like the creative life on the Left Bank along the Place Saint-Germain-des Près, or had the cozy places to gather, none as fine as Les Deux Magots, or the Café de Flore—nor was food as tasty as what was served at La Quatrieme République. ("Ah, that goddamn fine Jura pâté!") And why even try to compare the booze? The drink wasn't too good in New York in the 1920s, but we drank it, and the girls too. As some local poet was to write:

> Down south in Greenwich Village;
> Main Street maidens come for tillage...
>
> After each new thrill still racing
> Rarely chaste and always chasing.

Olga, who was reading Eliot's *The Waste Land*, said I wasn't only an uncouth Philistine, but also a dirty-minded licentious young man about poets. I told her I had met Tom Eliot through Ford Madox Ford, and no worse Jew-hating prig than old Tom was around. Olga said nonsense, but she had a Jewish grandmother and I could see she was worried; *The Waste Land* was so good that Eliot he just—she insisted—could not be such a horror. "You're always mocking genius. First Gene, now Eliot."

That broke us up for two weeks. I went to stay with a Tin Pan Alley songwriter who never had a hit, and ended by buying up downtown buildings falling apart, driving out the immigrants, renovating the wrecks and charging high rents.

The songwriter, when his first building was all rented, took me, Harold Stearns, and two men I never saw again, to the Pirates' Den and bought us all we could drink. "You mockies don't understand the Village is going to become a legend, and fake ones are the legends...I'm renting to advertising copy writers, *Saturday Evening Post* schmucks, Macy department-store buyers, interior decorators. All want a slam-bang Village address. So that weekends they can drink red wine, wear open shirts and talk about Russian ballet and Freud. Shows they're now just selling their souls for loot, letting their talents wither."

"Like their cocks," said Harold. "Waiter..." He pointed to his glass.

"You have to admit," said the songwriter/real-estater, "There is nothing more of a fake than this Village-Bohemian way of living. I just let in a cleaner class of posers."

Harold said, "Look, there's some good here too. The Boni Book Shop, and take Waldo Frank, Lewis Galantiere, Mumford, Deems Taylor."

I saw Olga at the other end of the place with an advertising man, Thorne S——. I went over and we had some drinks. I went home with Olga. We made it up fine and I promised to take seriously a magazine she was reading, *The American Mercury*, and wash up, if she did the cooking, and also change my smoking tobacco.

The truth is, the Village was in menopause—going into a change of life. The rich or the very successful were moving in—pressing out some of the lousy flea-bitten cold-water studio people. We'd go to a party in MacDougal Alley, and for the real Village, to the studio of Gertrude Vanderbilt Whitney, and to the studio of Jo Davidson making busts of all the millionaires.

I was getting ready to go back to Paris; it seemed most everybody was going, and I was given addresses to look up, and advice, and talking of the rate of exchange—"just dandy." My uncles' lawyers were going to give me enough from the trust to stay not too hungry in Europe. I said I'd go.

I put it to Olga. I asked her if she thought she could paint lampshades in Paris just as well as here in the Village. "And get more money because they'd be French imports."

She said, "I don't think I'd like living with you in Paris. You don't take seriously enough the cultural revolution going on."

I said I took it very seriously, I ate Gertrude's food, gave Ernest tips on the horse races. She hadn't heard of Hemingway. Olga was a culture vulture, like the intellectuals she followed what was new and stylish. She was running around with Bunny's crowd, and the Edna Millay group of people who got their names in the FPA column in the *World*.

With the promise of money I got from the family trust, and from three stories I had helped a pulp magazine writer with—as to plots about dogfights in the air with the German Red Ace in the late war, for half the payments for the stories—I had enough so Olga and I could live in Paris. She could stop painting snow scenes and sailing ships on fake parchment. "I don't know if I want to go with a man who writes for the pulps."

I said I wasn't a writer—didn't write for the pulps. I had just helped with details that would get us into a fairly good run-down apartment in Paris. I promised I wouldn't write or paint, or take any of the arts she loved, seriously. Olga said I could become a critic—they didn't have to know anything. We were both a bit crocked, and I said I thought she liked critics. Hadn't she been going around with the fat one?

She said maybe I was not really the only guy for her, but...which should have warned me. Because when I came back at four o'clock with two suitcases (I had cheap-talked them out of a pawn shop run by a Hudson Duster gang member who was part owner, he said, of the Hell Hole, a bistro on West Fourth, a real tough dive) one in each hand, and kicked open the door, there was the fat boy and Olga going at it on the studio bed, busy as a fiddler's elbow.

I threw the suitcases at them and went down to Naples Tony's speak and drank four awful slugs of what he said was the real Jersey lightning, an applejack that kicked like a mule. There was a playwright who was going out to Hollywood, so I let him buy the drinks and go on talking of getting it from Mable N——, the star. He said if you laid a woman with a sense of humor, you didn't end up feeling sad about copulation. Tony said if you were a Catholic, and your wife had a bambino every year, you never felt sad, "you feel plentiful about life." I ate a plate of pasta with clams and green sauce, and saw the playwright into a taxi and went back to our place. Olga met me at the door wearing long green-looking earrings. She said she was going to Paris with me—but I had to understand she was a free soul.

I said she could be free with anything she had, including her cunt. I began to pack one of the suitcases. She said I was a real true horse's prat Philistine after all. I asked her to say it again and when she did, I decked her. Lord, it felt fine. Right on the jaw. Olga was a hefty girl, mostly Swenski stock, with just one Jewish grandmother. I had been thinking for some time, big as she was, to let her have one on the chin. But I had to get over my upbringing and my family's tradition about the respect one owed to women. I left Olga staring in shock after me, and went to see about a berth on anything leaving for France and the Champs Élysées.

Midnight sailing on a French Line boat was a very posh event for many New Yorkers. Everybody coming down in top hats and evening gowns. Carrying bottles and flowers and even birthday cakes. Of course, that was the solid gold cigarette case (Dunhill's) first class, and the students going packed four to a cabin, everybody laughing and exchanging introductions. Also I was going on a ship that was not the *France*, but one of their lesser boats. There was no party of half-crocked friends to see me off, nobody to give me a party in the cabin below sea level I shared with two college boys from Princeton smoking pipes, and a leather-colored fat man from Tamaulipas in Mexico, who had bundles tied with heavy cords and kept brushing his moustache with his little finger, and looking at it in a little hand-mirror, as if to see if it was still there.

The boat was loaded with American students and people trying to act like students. They said it was exciting—golly—gee! Everybody, almost everybody, had a bottle or knew people who had one. Really going over on what the New York *World* writers called "the Big Pond." This traveling was a ritual all through the early 1920s. Flappers with long legs passed by, and a show girl for sure, peachy in furs and little hat with a sugar daddy—a packed cabin, all doing the Charleston. Men with smiles and cigars passing a bill to the steward for more ice. All the time you could smell the hothouse flowers dying, the bay's floating horrors. And some girls screaming or giggling. It was the same sound. And people being paged, music that might be French, a burst trunk. Parbleu!

I went on deck, elbowing people who said Jimmy Walker was on Board, Rudy Vallee, Miss America of last year. But none would take as unfashionable a boat as this, I was sure.

People below on the dock were shouting, people shouting back and some actor whose name I couldn't remember—he had a hairline moustache—Lowell something—being kissed by two girls and someone taking pictures of it. A long session of kissing and some reporter asking the actor something. But I was too far away to hear the answer. Anyway he wasn't sailing and left. It was very noisy, and someplace music was louder, and the gongs went around and the All Ashore.

I went down to the cabin and the two college boys were looking a little lost, their pipes had gone out. One wore golfing knickers and checked socks.

They asked me if I knew Paris. I said I had some knowledge of it. Did I know any writers there? I said I didn't know if I should admit it. I had been drinking. They were going to write. Writing is hard one of them said. I said I had heard it was hard work. I wasn't a writer myself. They said they were in their last year next year at Princeton, and did I know Scotty, a Princeton man they told me. I said I had exchanged words with him, been to a couple of parties at which he had been present. No, I didn't know Scotty too well. I knew Cole Porter, I said. But it seemed he was Yale, so they didn't ask for details.

The Mexican came back with a bottle and we drank from Lily cups. One of the college boys drank too fast, and I told him to get the hell out and not vomit in the cabin. We had to live in it nearly a week. By that time the All Ashore was long past and we were moving down the bay, rolling wickedly off Sandy Hook. The college youths, now mouth breathers, were unhappy. The Mexican, his name was Xesus Monterey Z——, took out a Colt .45 and said any puking college boy that puked in the cabin, he'd shove the pistol up his ass and pull the trigger, and he'd puke lead.

When the college boys were gone, we had a few more drinks and Xesus told me he raised commercial garden crops with peon labor in Marquez, and sold his crops to hotels all over the United States. They were not very good, but shipable early—and sold cheaply. He was going to Europe to find some cerrero American girl to make lof to. He was tired of fat Latin women with hairy armpits. I said there were American girls on the ship. He said si, yes, but he didn't have the courage to face them. On dry land he'd have the courage like a conquistador. He grabbed his left bicep and pressed. Si. Mas val tener que desear.

Xesus was a good cabin-mate. We drank ourselves to sleep. The Princeton boys had found sleeping space someplace else— where I don't know, for the ship was packed. Mostly Americans, mostly young. Up in first class the portly middle-aged and elderly moved about slowly, and Xesus wondered why they dared to travel, their bones seemed so brittle.

The food was only fair (it wasn't one of the crack ships of the line) but it was eatable and I ran up a bar bill (kept a nice glow—got a bar pallor, while others tanned). I didn't bother with the girls. I was feeling the after-effects of parting from Olga. I missed mostly our bickering, yelling at each other, the domestic fun of camping indoors with someone for several months. I think any close relationship with another human being is knowing to a fuller extent you're alive, even if you are annoying someone and they are annoying you. Yes, it's the human contact; it's being, it's existing. Those moments when it's all good between you. A laugh, a touch. Hell, it's right even just to be holding a match to her cigarette; it's as right as anything ever will be.

You get over it. You try to get over it. You insist on forgetting. You keep telling yourself it was all eyewash: she didn't use money wisely, she sucked her teeth, and when she brushed them she let toothpaste dribble down her chin, stain her robe. She was a status snob, felt she belonged to an overintelligent élite of Bohemian free livers. Yet when you held her close in the cold city night, and cats on the roof below yowled in love or hunger, and in the early morning the ash cans rattled—it was the good life. Morning closeness, eyes still sticky, it was warm and she was warm and you kissed her neck, groaning, got up to put on the coffee pot.

I wasn't any joy to myself on the trip over. I wondered where Europe would put all the Americans moving in migration back to where some grandpappy had come from. With a pack on his back or a sock of some embezzled funds or a younger son's share, with a kick in the ass; go make your fortune.

There was a cable dockside for me in Le Havre. SEND SHIP FARE JOIN YOU PARIS. OLGA. I didn't answer or send the money. I told myself I couldn't stand her brushing her teeth again every morning and the dripping paste down the front of her robe. I often lie to myself.

The Ravishing of Paris

I got back to Paris late in 1926, and it wasn't the Paris it had been. Even the Tzarist officers driving taxis were changed and La Stein had a new Panama hat. It was a three-ring circus. Ernest had published *The Sun Also Rises* and was enjoying fame and acting up as mean as always, only now with the foundation of success under his feet. You had to accept the real genius in him and overlook the obstreperous shitty side of him. Gertrude was already beginning to snipe at him—poor old La Stein, her tongue was hanging out for fame and popularity, and now Ernest had gotten it using all her prose ideas of short easy words repeated.

In re-creative writing she decided, as she told Elliot Paul, "You always draw pen lines in black and white in prose, the time of the times for heavy painted words in all colors these are now buried, buried away with Dickens."

There was lots of gossip and at the Flora, a lot more Americans, whole herds of them asking for Duff Twysden. Americans came on like a stampede, you stir them up one bit and they would run like a cattle drive down the boulevards. Their lifeline was the American Express where they replenished funds and met, exchanged blows and kisses and asked for the letter and money from home. They left the floor littered with discarded envelopes and were on their way to the Coupole for Pernod, apéritifs.

Paris was not, to us residue of old-timers, peaceful anymore; it was living in a public hallway. Every French Line boat disgorged more and more Americans, the boat trains ran hooting into the station. Out came the cheerful young; also middle-aged with big bellies; and the old and yellowed like whalebone carvings, muttering through their dentures, "Henry wouldn't have known the place...Edith says the Ritz is letting in *just* everybody." I suppose I felt squatter's rights, and I'd be thirty soon.

It was like a reverse migration of lemmings, Elliot Paul said. All kinds. College students, gash hounds, art lovers, would-be writers hugging their Corona portables, cocksuckers, vegetarians, the American Legion boys going bald. Lots of museum folk, fashion designers, con men, cardsharps (did I really see Nicky Arnstein with Robert McAlmon?) near the Opera. Mayor Jimmy Walker certainly, in Paris with a blonde, and Otto Kohn, an undersized shrimp of a banker, but a power in the arts. The Conde-Nast people were very elegant, very avant-garde and precious too. *Vanity Fair* gave America a peep into this new world.

Rents were up. At parties you were crowded by people you didn't care to meet with at parties. Negroes were cherished. Josephine Baker, and some said Jim Europe was in town, he who brought over le jazz with the AEF. But I never saw him. Still there were Americans who didn't write; only drank a litre of beer. They were beginning to look dusty to me.

More flappers were on the scene, more unbuckled overshoes on rainy days, more leg, slimmed-down ass, and no tits. They favored shingled hair and big green earrings. They had a limited vocabulary of ritzy, nifty, snazzy, the cat's pajamas, the bee's knees. Publishers, too, from New York, anteater-nosed, sniffing out manuscripts. After all, from Paris had come Joyce, now in the ninth edition, out of Sylvia Beach's Shakespeare & Co. And Ernest had hit, Scott had *Gatsby* out. You saw copies of *Gatsby* on the terraces of cafés, at hairdressers. There must be other goodies near the sawmill on the Rue Notre-Dame-des-Champs, the publishers felt. One knew the names of H. L. Mencken (who distrusted Paris beer), Liveright, Ben Huebsch and young B——, still referred to in party circles as Mr. Shit. All hoped to find another *Sun Also, Waste Land*. Gertrude was to settle for being the Earth Mother. She was working on another version of *Tender Buttons*, for *transition* was going to reprint it. Poor bitch. She felt neglected, and talk was that Ernest had been offered her body, for her first taste of cock, and he had turned her down. You could cut the literary gossip with a knife at any café, it was so thick. Some so rotten it had to be true.

There was no season of letup anymore. The Americans came in fall and in the winter. They were there before spring made the horse chestnut trees come around green. Even before the chairs were moved out on the terraces of the cafés.

Not all Americans gave a damn about books or art. There was a great visiting of old battlefield; Chateau Thiery, St. Mihiel, Sissone. The American Legion, other ex-soldier organizations came over in groups, to conventions, to drink, to overpay the whores, to play practical jokes, boast about production figures and their bootleggers. Also the greatness of Hoover, or was it Coolidge? The dead were not forgotten. Grave inspections, identifications, cemetery-site visiting were the fun journeys these ex-warriors delighted in. Although if you got three shots of Normandy apple brandy into some of them, they

confessed they had the "damn luck of just missing going over-
seas. From Hoboken. Waiting to board the transport and they
pull this Armistice thing on us."

They were thickening, and aging fast, the ex-soldiers, and
unlike the French and English, they seemed to have few legless,
armless, or half-faced survivors dying too slowly.

You could walk down some of the back streets, or through
little dog-soiled parks, and find the remains of the French victims of the Marne, of Verdun. The wreck in a wheelchair, turning his propelling levers with a claw of a hand, a face
half-covered with black cloth. The surgeon had not managed
to replace lost bone and tissue. And the ball-less. Jesus—there
they were—the creaking crabs with their cork and iron legs to
remind France it had been a shitty war as the profiteers passed
in their big cars. One flâneur told me if Baron Haussmann had
not made and paved the great boulevards, the street stones
would have been lifted up and barricades put up. Bullshit—
Paris wasn't that romantic anymore. The French only rebelled
against a small tip.

It was a city that Americans saw as living off the tourists.
Even the Germans were back with that extra fat gland on the
back of their short necks, by which one could identify them.
There were more Argentines and Greeks. Someone was faking
Matisse and Picasso, a sure sign, I felt, they had made it. I
remember a poor louse of a painter, Soutine. A dirty little fellow smelling—phew—of the carrion he painted, thick-lipped as
a minstrel nigger, always in pain with his gut. Some American
doctor who had invented a clap ointment, a Dr. B—— had
bought a lot of the artist's dead chickens and sides of beef pictures. Poor Soutine, he didn't know what the hell to do with
the wads of dough, and some said he burned most of it, but
I think the moochers and the whores he knew got a lot of it
in the cafés and estaminets.

I didn't know if I wanted to stay in this frenzied Paris. John was in Rome, and he had a girl named Brook; he ran an agency for some kind of American machinery tools. Brook? Girls' names were wonderful or nutty in the early 1920s. I knew a girl named Joy who came from Florida, who walked down Fifth Avenue one morning after a studio party, in a mink coat and nothing under it. And a solid one from Montana called Hope, who studied at Parsons and drew by dynamic symmetry—an art system. I knew two Dawns in Paris and several Fionas (from the Celtic of course). Also a Fawn who began a novel and never finished it. I loved its opening line: "'Shit,' said the Duchess." Later, someone else claimed that line, but Fawn wrote it first. She once also ate a fried egg with a shoehorn.

I made some extra money escorting American Legion brass to the various battlefields and burying grounds. Good food, big cars, lots of drink, and I nodded and toasted new versions of "American saved the bacon of these goddamn frog-eating sons-of-bitches, and you can't even get the right change back in any shop."

Bert and Allan were two American Legion men I liked whom I took on these tours. Both had been in the actual battles. If not in the line, as Bert put it, "We quartermasters, we got the chow and the ammunition and the toilet paper to them."

I had been reading Pepys' journals again, the best prose for hangovers I had found; and so for some time I sort of kept a journal myself. I still have some text of the talk of some of these ex-soldiers I took out to the battle sites. Bert and Allan were not bad guys. It came clear that the war had been the one great big adventure of their lives. They had gotten a big dose of the Old Nostalgia for their army days, and forgotten the mud, the cooties, the rotting bodies, and the butcher-shop smell of dressing station blood.

Allan: "Just look at them buildings." Bert: "Slow pokes. They haven't fixed up things. You still see the ruins."

We were all in a big hired Caddy, drinking cognac from a
bottle, even André, our driver. Allan liked the French and
admitted to André, "Boo coo, I mean your butter, you can't,
gosh no, get sweet butter like it in Newark, no matter at what
price. And the bread. I mean so what the hell—some of the
French, they don't bathe."

André reached for the bottle. Allan nodded, "Now you
take the Heinies. Was in Berlin last year. Could eat pancakes
and maple syrup right off the sidewalks, that clean. But you
gotta remember they were the enemy. Never any trouble with
the plumbing in the Kraut crapper. Now the hotel I'm at with
Bert—in Paris, mind you—on what the hell, roo-Saint-
something, they got old shit saved up there in the john they
been hoarding since Napoleon had the trots."

André said, "Merde."

"That's the word, *that's* the word. You in the war, André?"

"Fuk la war."

Once, just once, I was short-order cook at an American
Legion picnic in the Chemin des Dames section, an "All American Style Picnic." No French food. Franks, chili, hamburgers,
cole slaw, steaks, pies, ice cream. We ran out of bread, we were
short of lettuce, a half a leaf on a sandwich had to do. The ham
slices were divided. The noise of dancers under the trees, and
at the tables and those seated on the grass, mixed with the rattle of dishes. It was mind-destroying.

I had six farm girls working and I was slicing, patting, frying, grilling, scrambling—sticking the pimentoed olive crucified
on a toothpick into the triple-decks, pulling around pans of sizzling bacon, dishing out egg salad on a layer of bread, adding
a fistful of potato chips, the sliver of dill pickle—until I ran out
of decor items. From then on it was just ham and franks,
nothing else. On any type of bread we had. "They want fancy
fodder, eat at the Ritz." By twelve, all the clam chowder pots
were empty.

I was too bushed—we all were—to add more gallon cans to heat. The barbecue sauce on the Texas-style ribs had been watered once too often. I was tossing in dry onion powder, mustard powder, Lea & Perrins as a sop sauce. Half an hour before twilight, I put my head under a cold water faucet and imagined I was dead on the sea bottom.

Up and Down and Low

Without Bugles

I got to like Bert and Allan more and more. Maybe because, poor bastards, they were like I would have been after my knobby adolescence, if I had gone into the family plants. Not that I was much of anything better—touting AEF battlefield tours. I just felt Bert and Allan were decent folk really; tainted maybe, harassed by their families, the demands of their wives for the good living, the better car, a fur coat. So as we did the battlefields, crossing the Aisne, going to see the graves by Mont Blanc, walking through what had once been Belleau Wood where *Les Américains*, our guide happily recalled, had really "died in large numbers."

I saw maybe we were all wrong, we expatriates in Paris. We who sneered at the Berts and Allans, Joes, Jakes, and Willies, the Harrys who stayed home in the USA, worked too hard, waxed shiny cars, ate cornflakes, raised up baseball-playing kids. And yet these folk dreamed of coming to Paris and maybe catching up on something they had missed in the war, seeking—as who the hell wasn't?—some responsive twitch from the universe.

Or perhaps I was feeling this seizure of doubt because I was drinking their booze, eating their food, riding in their hired car, and so was I kissing ass? When we stood by the graves of some of those nearly half million British youths who died between the 1st and 3rd Ypres, Bert was crying and Allan was trying to whistle with dry lips. All the graves we saw had no red poppies growing between the cement crosses and some Stars of David. I got this nervous contraction of my face muscles I once had flying the war.

Bert had been with the 26th Division at Seichprey, I found out, and Allan was with the 1st, north of Cantigny. I suppose, for the first time since 1918, I thought of it as my war too, me as that callow kid in air bases. Going up in the morning to fly over the lines and below me a few million unlucky pricks, like the two men I was escorting to the remains of what Bert said was "the last of all major wars." I said sure, I didn't see how the fat pricks who ran the world could ever get any other pricks stupid enough to fight the wars for them again. We were drinking Three Star out of the bottle. André, polishing the hood of the car, said with a wink, "Tout le monde la bataille!" I explained to Bert and Allan the French were a cynical race and Bert said that we'd "pulled their ass out of the fire for the last time." That finished the bottle.

André had a St. Christopher medal buried in chest hair, and he drove us over to Verdun, we singing the old songs "Madelon," "Mademoiselle from Armentieres," although I don't really believe they were ever sung as often as sentimental people thought they were. Verdun is a delight for tourists. The place was still torn up in parts; huge cement soldiers five times life size were set up as monuments—waving themselves on to glory. Also rusting bayonets in the earth still showing hidden bodies where a trench had caved in. There were stands where you could buy German helmets and moldy leather belts with Gott Mit Uns buckles, regimental badges and brass shell casings as ash trays.

André farted at the memorial to Petain, "Saviour of Verdun."

"The murdering swine. The soldiers went into battle baa-baaing like sheep to show they were being butchered. When some refused, driven mad by hopeless attacks, the cocksucker Petain, he took every tenth Frenchman in the sector and shot him. Some he blew to bits with cannon. To a heroic France, à bonne bouche!" André lifted one leg and farted loud and clear again. We all joined in cheerfully like a glee club among the bones. I don't suppose it really mattered, for the war was being romantically written about with sentimentality and sobs. How sad, how too young to die. Ernest has been working on one such book, I hear.

We got back to Paris, Bert with a bad cold, and I had just about decided to go someplace else. Paris was becoming a suburb of places I didn't care for. It wasn't Main Street or Babbittland because I saw merits in Main Streets, and the little fat butterballs of its slob businessmen, even if it wasn't the fashion to like them. I always felt Sinclair Lewis really was a Main Street Babbitt himself, just mocking his image in the distorted mirror. I felt the writers who felt above the main streets, stank. But then I wasn't writing for the little magazines thinking Stalin was all...

Red, or Hal (never Sinclair) when in Paris was a drunken elf with scar tissue for a face, and always gabbing, acting the nut and giving out with dialogue that no American ever spoke. I never could understand how people thought Hal had an ear for real talk. I knew village and city Americans and how they really sounded, and no one spoke like a Sinclair Lewis character, only Red himself. But I liked Hal, and he would buy the drink when we freeloaders at Jimmy's, Harry's were broke.

Many people I really grew to dislike. What helped give me that final shove to leave Paris were Gertrude and Alice, and the circle of hand-holding fairies around them. There were some opinions passed on about her nasty, bitchy cult, and on Gertrude herself, as a slob, and worse, a fraud. Many other people who made opinions were being bamboozled by her. You either kissed her tail, the boys on the *Trib* or *Herald* said, or you loathed her. She was always pushing homosexual love and games, and if you spoke up, as one American did, for Ma and Pa fucking, she gave out how nobody was really straight, and we all wanted to be dykes or sissies. Someone said she had more prick than her male circle. Lots of people began to dislike her more and more, but the real horror to most not in the fan club, was Pussy (as Alice Toklas was called by Gertrude; Gertrude was Lovie—but maybe I have it the wrong way round). Alice looked, Ernest said at Jimmy's bar one night, "like a kosher Indian's miscarriage." Alice really ruled Gertrude, giving out one of those side glances of rancour—and you could see she was putting the boot to Gertrude. I think Gertrude enjoyed playing the little girl being brutalized by Alice; some half-assed exquisite agony of sadistic pain. Gertrude had a hell of an idea about herself as a genius. She hated Joyce's success, and Ernest's too. She liked to place herself, I remember, with Poe and James (William, I think) and Whitman, and with a song, "The Trail of the Lonesome Pine." Elliot Paul plugged her in the *Tribune*. But I saw her as a hoax, self-perpetuated by males still seeking Mom's tittie. An affection made into a literary cult by her flap-wristed young men and butchy women. "By 1940, I'm sure no one will remember her," Leo, her brother told a doctor I knew.

Once I took a Stanford professor out to the Marne battlefields. Had a son killed someplace nearby in the war—body never found. In the afternoon, after viewing the city from the dome of the Sacré-Coeur, we returned to the Continental to find the lobby area all in total darkness. The electrical system had failed all over the hotel this time, not just in the guests' rooms. Dr. P——, the economist-philosopher, and I retired to the open-air bar in the courtyard and drank beer while electrical experts rushed around hunting the power failure. The professor smiled. "Never trust scientists. They begin with the cotton gin and end up with the TNT or worse. Besides, Paris, my wife thinks, is best by candlelight. At least those parts we outlanders see. Look at those women, marvelous—a little too much behind and nothing missing in front. Paris is worth seeing."

I said what the Paris visitors see is a mere surface stirring, a shallow floating through hotels and shops no Frenchman in his right mind would come near. I explained the traveler lives in a Paris made just for him, set with beartraps and charmers. Not the true city or the native life. Dr. P—— agreed that we are isolated in a false world. "A small little New York, if an American, a bit of London, if from Great Britain; even an Arab section exists." He added he had observed the American traveler doesn't put his shoes out at night to be shined, but at breakfast insists on cornflakes, bran, the Paris edition of the *Tribune*. "The average traveler speaks almost no French, expects the hotel staff, the shopkeeper, the taxi driver to understand English. Is it possible under such conditions to fully know a city?" I said yes, and no. And pointed out Colette and Utrillo, but these meant nothing to them. "How 'bout Josephine Baker?"

Truth is, there is more than a Paris frivolous, lewd, vicious, cruel. There is a Paris of Mama, Papa, Grandpère, little Georges who peepees on the park grass. Those of us who have managed to see a bit of French Paris—visited its fringes—know how much the hurried visitor misses. To the travelers, Paris is often sleek, cantankerous, sly. Yet there is a Paris of loyalty, magnanimity, compassion. I know it's there some place.

Dr. P—— asked what does the American living in Paris think of the French? Do the French they know have the true zest for life of folk, say from St. Joe, Missouri, or Elkhorn, Michigan? Are they perceptive, sensitive organisms as they cheat one in the rate of exchange; have they real values, sensibilities, as they palm off some trash of meubles d'occasion as a rare antique? Dr. P—— was certainly a searching fellow.

I said what I have caught of the true French, what penetration I have made into French family life, seems to indicate they, like ourselves, are troubled by not being able to live at their fullest potential. They, too, if thinkers, see life as a kind of caricature that is accepted as a picture of society, are aware of their greed for money, the cruelty of national grabbing that distorts the real world.

Dr. P—— sat sipping his beer. He thought, spoke: "The real world? Even in Paris it doesn't exist; in a way it's a fraud, a hoax of bankers, politicians. Of you writers, priests and songmongers. You offer the clichés of a society huddling under a leaking umbrella called the Western World. Take our own American social structure..."

I was happy when the lights came back on. I have no interest in facts and figures, no grasp of historical generalization. My world exists in my skin, and the skin of those I touch.

On the way up to Dr. P——'s room, in the elevator, he was frowning. "Your poor Parisian is in the same trap the rest of us live in. We are all that lethal species with its finger on the trigger."

"Bad as that?" I smiled. I was going up to be paid off for three days as a guide.

"I'm just trying to express why we can't penetrate deeply into the real Paris."

I said, "Too bad."

"How deep, for that matter, have any of our big mouths penetrated into American life? Emerson, Teddy Roosevelt, Brisbane."

(I wondered if I'd get a five-dollar tip.)

"Basically, my grandfather said, we're a decent people."

"We Americans are a predatory society. We consume world resources. So why should the French let us into their lives?"

I felt enough soft soap for me for one day. "We're going sailing on the Seine at ten o'clock tonight."

He gave me ten dollars above the price agreed upon. I paid up some back rent and bought a cane once owned by Zola. To remember Paris.

Goodbye Again?

So the idea of leaving Paris wasn't too painful, but I can't blame it all on Lovie and Pussy. The trouble was that I had been trying to get a stake for travel by gambling on the market at Heinz & Co. on the Rue Cambon. Also betting bigger on the horses, by which it should not be too hard to make money, as the tracks around Paris are the most crooked in the world except for the horse races run in Mexico. The jocks and hot walkers could let you in on a boat ride, as a fixed race was called, for a share of your winning tickets. It wasn't only the jocks. The owners—English lords, Corsican gangsters, Greek arms merchants, French automakers, wine growers, packing-house sausage stuffers—all had racing stables and some set up races.

You had to be in the right place at the right feed box, be sure you had the right nag at Longchamps for the Grand Prix or the Omnium Handicap. Coming around to the finish line, the jocks who had set up a French boat ride all had tickets on the one horse in their boots, so you almost hear the brakes scream as they pull in their mounts to let the winner go through.

I knew this little old former English jockey, Mick—now a stable hand—who had been run off the English tracks when he helped get Tod Sloan, the American jockey, to agree to the pulling of the King's horse that Sloan was riding in the Derby. No American has since been permitted to race on an English track. Mick was one of the wide ones (wise insider) in the paddocks, who gave Ernest's and Elliot's pals tips. If you brought him a bottle of Marc, he'd maybe give you the feed-line talk on what race was a sure thing. The English-language newspapers in Paris had their horse handicappers, but I never took much stock in them, as they were usually broke, mooching drinks. I preferred Mick. This meet, the Prix Vermeille, was attracting big crowds, and I went out with some people from Bricktop's saloon and some of the General Motors European crowd. They had good comfortable cars and treated me right because they knew I had this source of race information. The French were just beginning to use the battery on the horses, which was a metal thing attached to a car battery that gave a horse a good jolting set of shocks when placed on whatever genitals he had left, just before the race. If the jock could hold the panic-stricken animal at the gate, the horse in fear of more battery would run his heart out, race horses being as neurotic as writers.

I had borrowed and lost a few hundred on the stock market; I needed a big winner. It was a beautiful day, the grass green as goose turd, and the sky a painter's blue. I was betting all I had again borrowed on Mick's advice, to back a horse I shall call here, Fait Accompli; the owner is a very powerful industrialist, and so if I identified the horse, he could send a couple of Sicilians with knives after Mick, even me. At least I heard he did things like that. One of the girls, once at the Capucines Revue, now only has one eye left.

Mick was feeling no pain when I saw him in the paddock before the big race. I had a press pass borrowed from someone at Jimmy's Bar. Mick had been sampling a bottle I had left for him, and he was all screwed up with Cockney laughter and weaving his head about, a head that looked like an Idaho spud forgotten all winter in the dark. He waggled a finger at me from behind a stack of oat bags.

"A ruddy marvel 'ats what it is. Shsss...now lad I'm just letting a few close chaps in..."

"Still Fait Accompli?"

"Would I, mate, be lyin' to ya? Owner 'imself has a packet on the bugger. Been keeping the 'orse under wraps like, see? Never let 'im out in gypsy tracks. It's good odds, 32 to 1. Ruddy marvel of a race. Git your money up, Gov. And remember ole Mick give it to ya."

"Look, Mick, I'm putting everything—and it's borrowed—but my gold inlays on this race. I need money. You're damn sure, Mick? The race is—?"

"Go put the family jools up the spout. Place yer bet."

Which I did, and had two brandies to steady myself. In the grandstand—fashion models on parade, expensive whores, made it a Dufy picture, which I had never believed before. There was Coco Chanel with some attending Englishmen, and a herd of the Elsa Maxwell zombies, also bankers and publishers and Americans, the usual Argentines and Greeks, and thousands of others, but I didn't bother to count. People were drinking Chambolle-Musigny and cheering. It was to be a race on grass. The horses came out. A German said to me, "Unglaublich." Fait Accompli was a big black brute of a horse, with a monkey-sized jockey in racing silks on his back. Tod Sloan had changed riding styles in Europe. Mick has told me Sloan taught the jocks to ride standing, leaning over the horse's neck, and with a very short stirrup strap on one side, which helped them working around on an oval track.

It was a fine race meet, I felt, and I was delighted that at last horse racing had become a science, and that stables and jocks had taken to winning in turn and didn't depend on chance or skill. Coming around the last turn it was my horse up front, and the odds had gone up five points on the tote listings.

Coming close to the finish, Fait was on the outside and pumping himself half a length in front—at which point the jock stopped whipping and a gray horse came up and across the finish line. I knew I had been jobbed, and people cried "Merde alors!" It was a swindle. I was too low to see I was a swindler myself, depending on secret information of a fixed race.

I went to one of the bars and some winner was buying Chablis Vaudesir. I wondered how I'd get back to Paris; I had informed two of my party to bet on F.A. "Secret...can't fail...a real fix..." I wouldn't want to face them. Then there was the rent unpaid, my debts, and eating until I got my check in three weeks from the States. I owed people about eight hundred dollars.

Ned B—— who taught drawing at Parsons' Paris art school came by, counting franc notes and asked me why my tail was dragging, and I said that my jaw was on the ground, not my keister. He said too bad. He'd had this solid tip from a wop hot walker working in the paddocks (a hot walker cools off horses after a run by walking them around). And so Ned had made a packet. He offered to take me to Paris and lend me some money. Ned was a good guy and in love with his wife, and even in Paris went to church on Sundays—St. Joseph's—English services. He was one of the most decent men I knew, and I've known more than you would think. Only they've had little effect on my life. We were finishing a drink when there was a commotion outside and the sound of people running, and then some car sirens. A girl I knew who was supposed to be the niece of Nina, Leo Stein's off-and-on mistress, came by. I asked her:

"What's the uproar?"

"Somebody just shot at a bloody jockey out back. Something about a double-cross." It was a miss, and two men from Belgium, smugglers, gossip said, were held for a little time. There was never any mention of the shooting as an assassination attempt. I think one French sports paper ran a few lines about a jockey cleaning a gun, not knowing it was loaded. But I didn't see the item myself. The French are great sports lovers and don't do anything if they can help it to give the impression, in print, that "le sport" could be tainted.

That was how I got strapped in debt, became desperate—and moved in as household companion of Fran. She was—once—at the turn of the century—the mistress of a Chicago financier and notorious grain speculator. Now she was paid so much a year to live abroad. She also had a rich portfolio of streetcar stocks. Fran was fat, a pink porky plumpness, chemical-colored hair. She was no longer young, and she liked young men who could make her laugh—laugh and do small services for her. I don't like the expression *kept man* or *gigolo*. I tried to think of myself as an attendant, say a male personal maid assisting her toilet. And getting Fran out of her bath was like landing Moby Dick.

I will say this about Fran; she was the only one who helped me when I got into trouble with the French idea of justice. I had been down on my luck, as I've pointed out, from horserace bets that went very wrong and playing the game of the stock market. I was down to living in a sleazy hotel room with a Bible pounder named Tommy, a Texan who spent late night hours street preaching some kind of Baptist faith as a sure way to salvation. Tommy was a nice old missionary coot. His French was a bad as his teeth and his badly fitting salt-and-pepper wig. The night people of Paris—mostly shady customers—were not ready for the one true religion, not from an old man who stood on street corners and talked in some dialect not at all amusing.

I was writing a series of letters to the lawyers of the family trust, to try and wangle some needed advances on the money they paid me. Tommy had a small stone-age typewriter which the landlord had taken as a pledge against the rent Tommy owed him. The missionary society back in Texas was behind with his missionary pittance.

Tommy borrowed back the machine and I typed my letters and borrowed some stamps and sent them off at three-day intervals, so they'd bombard the lawyers with the desperation of my situation.

One morning I woke up to find a note from Tommy. He had just heard about Hyde Park corner near Marble Arch in London, and was off to use the free speech privileges offered there.

I figured I had better leave the hotel in a day or two. The next day two police came to see me and asked for my carte d'identité. Tommy had gone off with the typewriter. But I had used it last, and I was the thief, the landlord insisted. I said nonsense, and the flics nodded, and one said, "Property is property."

So I was carried off by the police who said, "Do not worry. It is a small matter."

It was no small dream, but a cold dirty jail I found myself in. Locked up in a small smelly cell, I had time to think out what I had heard of French justice; prisoners had no inalienable rights. French law is now worse than most of the police and legal procedures in Europe, with the exception of England which is closer to the American idea you are innocent until proven guilty. The French system leans more to you being guilty, then *you* try to prove you are not. There is no coddling of prisoners, no respect for legal rights; mostly it is just being kept locked in jail until your trial. Balls-scratching jailers, no heat, a great deal of red tape, paper work, a fat group of bored officials all trying to hold on to their own departments until pensions were ripe. All set in cold indifference to the prisoner. I began to hope the pansy I knew in the U.S. Embassy was not on vacation. (He was.)

In the morning a Citroen police car took me to the Prefecture building on the Ile de la Cité. "Slowness is beauty," Rodin once said. French justice is slow, but not beautiful. Waiting for questioning I sat in a small cell, no hurry anywhere all along the line.

I was asked to sign a form. I said, "Non—no." But I signed instead of taking a beating. Held incommunicado, I could call neither some lawyer nor the American Embassy. An Embassy— unless one knew top brass there—is seldom known to break its neck hurrying to help Americans not famous out of trouble. As for a lawyer, the answer "oui, oui," was all I got there in the freezing cold, the stink of old cells.

As I went back to prison, the landlord said he had found the typewriter in a pawnshop. Pawning a stolen machine, tut, tut.

In the afternoon, handcuffed, I was taken to be photographed and fingerprinted, after which I was moved into a holding tank full of real scum, hard-eyed hoods. There was no plumbing, but just a hole in the floor, and near it an old vag sat, eating a chunk of stale bread. The stink was strong and climbing higher.

Next day I was handcuffed and placed in the unique Paris police van, an Iron Maiden on wheels. Each prisoner sits in a kind of personal coffin or wooden grave, isolated and very much alone. Each coffin is locked from the outside. I laughed all the way to the Fresnes prison outside of Paris, as I was close to total nuttiness—laughing stiffened my need for survival.

They took my belt, watch, money, a racing form, shoelaces,

nail file, two love letters, then pushed me into an icy cell. French prisons do not have heat or luxury cells along the lines of the American palaces for prisoners. The frugal French prisons are mainly to punish, as I found out in a lacerating few days—not to entertain by craft arts, radio, or movies. There was no working plumbing, not even a boîte à l'ordure in our cell. For I was in with six fellow mugs, and all were amused at my story of the pawned typewriter. They agreed with me as to the inequities of the outside world.

We freezing bastards slept on straw, rose at seven-thirty; no belt and shoelaces meant one held up one's pants and shuffled along to walk. Food was shit—dog dung, served from big garbage cans. Bread, not the fine French stuff, and wet rust passed for coffee. At noon, la soupe, a thick paste of pulped, rotten vegs and potatoes like wallpaper glue. At ten-thirty lights out; came the scratching, the hawking, the buggery, blowing of lovers. On the fourth day, my name was called. I was to go on trial—a crime against property. So again the coffin wagon to the Ile de la Cité, to the Palais de Justice. I thought of that old lithograph print, the one of the prisoner strangling under the gag as the judge announces, "The accused will now have his say."

I waited all day in a cell or in court, but my name was not called and I went back to prison. A prisoner, Jules, who sold pictures of real kittens as dirty postal cards, was leaving the prison and he promised to take my name to the embassy and to a lawyer I knew in Paris. He was a well-dressed gambler in my cell and said, while justice couldn't be hurried in a case, I had a simple miscarriage of justice. It wasn't my typewriter, and I hadn't pawned it had I? So? Don't worry.

When the gambler left—he said his freedom cost his petite one a good-sized bribe to the mistress of a leading liberal politician—he left me a pack of French cigarettes which are punishment for anyone. Three days after the gambler left, my trial came up. René, the French lawyer I knew, had gotten Fran to pay him a retainer. René wasn't a very good lawyer, but he was the only one I knew. He took small cases like representing Americans who had their baggage damaged, been in a fight with a taxi driver, punched a waiter in the nose. His hopes were to become a rich divorce lawyer for Americans who came to Paris for a separation, a divorce, nearly legal in the United States. I told René I knew Dudley Field Malone, the big American divorce lawyer, and I'd introduce him if he'd get me off. He said it was a bagatelle. In the courtroom he got the case dropped on some simple facts: I had not owned the typewriter, had never pledged one to the landlord, and had not been the one who pawned a typewriter. Besides the landlord had the machine in question in his possession. René added some words that I was a hero, had fought and bled for France in the skies, and was a valid hero and he produced a batch of medals—not mine, I saw at once—decorations which he claimed I had been awarded by various grateful nations, including three by the French. He saluted me and sat down.

So a free man, and needing a bath, shave, and some clean clothing free from jail lice, I moved in with Fran, wondering if I would not have been better off in prison...foolish thought.

Fran's World

My life in the big apartment on the Rue Jacob with Fran was, I suppose, the low point of my low life. Fran was cheerful, boozy and smoked Primrose or Gitanes Vizars. She was not stingy, but demanded thanks. In her early seventies at least, was still sensual and given to talking of her youth while sipping Dry Monopole. "Oh, it had been a grand life on the Cunarders and always the best suites at the grand hotels all over Europe. Kerist, it was the gay life, Bertie's yachting parties and James Gordon Bennett and his parties, such divertissements. It isn't the same anymore. Crass now, chéri, everything crass as a bucket of spit."

Bertie was, I gathered, King Edward, son of Victoria, and Fran—had she really been part of that crowd, the Stanford White crowd? Certainly the old poops remembered her as part of the sinful American colony before the Great War, and along the Riviera. You could almost smell Berry Walls's cigars and Edith Wharton's scent in Fran talking about the fin de siècle hell raising.

Fran was vicious without being cruel—she was heavy now and a bit wrinkled, but game. Smoked a little too much, ate too much, was amorous as a mink. She favored feathered dressing robes and the best champagne. There was a cook and maid and two smelly little dogs who peed, when excited or scolded, on the rare rugs.

I liked Fran when she was swacked, liked hearing about Paris as it was before my time there, getting all the old gossip about Paris Singer and Isadora Duncan. Louis Comfort Tiffany, and the real people Proust based his characters on.

We'd get loaded on brandy after a night at the Scheherazade or Ciro's, and fall into the big bed that was sworn to Fran by an antique dealer as once belonging to Cora Pearl, a grand courtesan of the Second Empire, "Être cousin d'argent." Once or twice a night I'd have to help her to the bathroom to flush her kidneys, and she was a great weight and hardly fully awake, or sober either. In the end I went to the Flea Market and bought her a huge chamber pot and told her it had once belonged to the original of the Dumas fils characters miscalled Camille. Which was a lie, but it was a way of getting Fran to squat and me not have to get up and drag her to the bathroom, risking a hernia.

We were a nice friendly couple. We ate well. We fed like pigs, in fact. Every good restaurateur knew us. A 'Homard, Vieux Logis, Maxims. The maître d' always saw we got the best and what was special. "The only way to go," Fran would say over homard aux aromates, or faison Souvarov. "Eat yourself to death, chéri. I want to go out full of pâté and roast goose, and smelling of truffles." We certainly used the knife and fork and sipped the Madeira followed by the bubbly.

After which we'd go to some night spot, the Capucines Revue, the Florida, Bricktops, and I'd trot her out on the dance floor before the hooch hit us hard. Around two a.m., we'd get helped out to a taxi, handing out franc notes to the staff, and go to the flat. Just about make it to our second floor and begin to strip. Leaving a trail of shoes, stockings, her corset, panties, my waistcoat, jacket, socks, like an Indian raid. We never really remembered dropping into the bed to cork off. Paris night life for the well-off left one bushed.

I must say we were good solid sleepers. No one dared pull the curtains apart till about noon; the bedroom smelling like early morning Mass. Cécile, the maid, an old sourpuss from Savoy, would stick her head in and if Fran was stirring, moaning, or kicking off the covers, Cécile would bring in the big tray of coffee and rolls and the country butter, the raspberry jam. I'd have one cup in two gulps, and go down the hall to the guest bathroom and do the morning indecencies, shave, if not too shaky, shower, hold my head and take some hangover pills with a glass of Contrexeville mineral water. I'd have remorse, regret, and shake off despair with three fingers of cognac.

Fran came out to a real breakfast-lunch combined, still in a dressing gown, hair up in a net. "Don't look close at me you sonofabitch, just pass the kippers...courage sans peur."

We'd have besides kippers, sometimes bacon and eggs, quiche Lorraine, pâté de poisson, sometimes grilled sweetbreads, usually an assortment of dishes. Émile, the chef, would be trying out coquille di Cap Canaille, a dessert of soufflé Misiral or Chocho. "A woman cook isn't worth a damn," Fran insisted. "Kerist knows, men are the best cooks. Émile, what's for tea?"

He'd rattle off some items—biscotti, Bavarois rubane. I'd go dress, pick out a cane. I was a great cane man—Beauge's had a fine collection—and *what* hat? The bowler, the snap brim, the fancy dago hat from Rome with a furry finish? *Which* spats? Problems of the day. The taxi would be waiting around three and we'd do the shops. We didn't—either of us—give a shit about art galleries, concerts, the opera, or gatherings of intellectuals, unless Diaghilev was there; Fran adored him. If there was a good American film, we'd pop in and hold hands and share a box of chocolates Around five, we'd have some cocktail party. We'd avoid the writers' parties, publishers' shindigs. Fran liked movie stars being welcomed, some party of an international stock market swindler promoting match stocks or oil bonds. We'd greet friends at dress designers' little affairs, pansy interior decorators bringing together the smart new people, some of whom said they knew this new chap, Noll Card. And what niggrah stud was schtupping Nancy, and did H. G. Wells really have skin that tasted of honey, and was he as horny as they said with Elizabeth of the German Garden? It was detailed gossip Fran liked; drinking, nodding, patting my arm, her hair all a brass-and-gold coiffeur, topped by a marvelous turban, deep in her furs; we shopped at Yendis, Greco, Chantal. Fran's legs were still very good, knockers held up in harness and her voice a big booze-rasped but amused. You could still sense what a beauty she must have been without the lard she now carried, before the wrinkles and the sags and teeth needed all that special attention.

It was the martini era, and champagne of course. We only nibbled the tidbits of sea life, and fish entrails, sturgeon's eggs on fingernail-sized toast.

We'd go back to the flat and maybe have a tea and a sandwich or two; mousse à l'Ananas or just thin ham and cold grouse. I was gaining weight like a retired jockey. I had to charge suits and a dozen Sulka shirts to Fran's account, as my shape changed. I was expanding so, I didn't know who was in my mirror. Fran would put on a sleeping mask and ear plugs as the street lights went on: "Sleepy time, bye-bye."

I would move to the guest room and brood, and figure out how to steal enough money to get away to Rome.

Fran would be up by eight, as the dinner-time traffic got started—she growling, thumping her chest to get up the sleepy times slimes, swearing and reviving herself with a cordial or Bristol Cream. We'd get into our evening clothes and go out to dinner at some fancy place. Usually with "our gang," people of the theatre and cinema, vaudeville or the halls. I remember Pearl White, the serial queen, some Tin Pan Alley song publishers, Fanny Ward, somebody called Glaenzer, a Chicago utility wizard, circus performers, a charming cardsharp who worked the ocean liners, and, I gather, had been Fran's lover twenty years before. He now had an Italian wife who gestured with her hands and kicked him under the table but usually wounded other guests. Once it was Mr. Hearst joined us, and Marion Davies and party, and a second-string Rothschild—they breed a lot of nobodies. It was certainly not an intellectual group, "our gang." But practically everybody had gold cigarette cases and some wore jewels with untrue histories. "Kerist, Catherine the Great must have had six necks for all the jewels they sell here as hers, chien."

In company, Fran was very refined. She said *sheet*, not shit— she said *pussy*, not cunt, and she used *dong* for cock, *Schtupp* for fuck. At least with Elsie de Wolfe, the Agha Khan, Lady Mendl, Fanny Ward.

Of course, after a dinner, all the food and the wine and brandy, no one wanted to go home to sleep—"Stops the heart, sleeping on food." So it was the night clubs. If the Prince of Wales really played the drums, we never caught the act, and Babette, the boy from Texas, who did a female on the high wire was always the same. Fran liked his gowns. So, as I've pointed out, two or three in the morning, full of the rich chow, lousy night-club champagne—after midnight I was sure they were just selling labels and alcohol and cider, back to the flat and bed. And so on and so on. Week after week, and month after month.

Being a kept man is an art I just didn't have. I liked to sit alone on a café terrace and read of the world going to hell in the newspapers in three languages. I didn't like the afternoon movies. Clara Bow and Joan Crawford weren't my ideals. I also wasn't that mad about gourmet food in such huge portions as Fran and I packed away. There came that moment when the maître d' set fire to the orange brandy under the crêpes, and I broke into a cold sweat, and was short of breath.

Also Fran was beginning to treat me like a servant. She'd snap at me while nibbling a huge chocolate bon bon, she spread out on the bed, "In the saddle, sonny," or "dive, chéri." What really brought it all to a climax was the morning I had trouble bending over to button my spats. My belly got in the way. I had three pairs of spats, pearl gray, pale lemon, and a slate-blue set. The room went round and round as I tried to get at the buttons.

I had charge accounts, but no money. And I needed money for escaping. I went to six of the best shops: Old England, Willoughby's, d'Ahetze, Brennans, a few others, and I ordered a few thousand franc's worth of haberdashery, assorted cuff links, tie pins, studs, shirts. Then I'd make a deal where I could with some manager to sell it all back to them for half, for cash. They'd still collect the full bill from Fran. Managers of shops are often very understanding. This took time, and I had so little free time. It was hard to get away from Fran's demand on my time and body. "Never de trop dear boy, never de trop." She'd add in her dreadful French, "De rigueur."

Waiting for her with other gigolos at some fashion show or shop—Paquin's, Tecla's, Yendis—for the ladies to decide or not to decide what they liked, or did not, I'd look around at the kept men. Christ, what a crew, I thought—most of them years in the trade. Faces and eyes made up, a wig here and there, the sag of a rice-powdered chin line, the too-well-cared-for nails. And the silver bracelets set with watches; slave bracelets for sure. I got to know them: there was Tony who serviced an American opera star; Ferde who was double-gaited on call to an heiress from England; Tristan who served both an American lady race stable owner *and* her husband, a baron. And Chass who just waited for those two summer months when a popular *Lady's*

Home Journal serial writer came to Paris. She did a pure moral prose blessed by book clubs and the YMCA. She came over, the Paris *Herald* wrote, "to meditate on her next uplifting story." She holed up in a hotel in the Rue La Fontaine, spent the two months with two whores and Chass, and assorted tools for inflicting pain. After this, a week with Chass at some health resort like Baden Baden—then sailing for home and the moral prose.

I really was all sweat and bile that afternoon as I looked over these poor bastards, gigolos smelling of scent, Turkish cigarettes, and stale socks. Europeans, some of them were not given to too much bathing.

I figured it out right in front of Tecla's; if I could get a couple of thousand dollars ahead in my trading-post swindle, I'd get away one night and leave most of the wardrobe. It wouldn't fit me anyway after I stopped wallowing in the rich swill. I was over 230 pounds, and had always been, for all my height, under 180. I yelled right out, "C'est bien ça!"

Fran was busy ordering the apartment to be done over. She did the place over every year. One year all white, Elsie de Wolfe in charge, then all black glass and black marble by the man who had created Van Dongen's dining room, and now the cutey French period was going. Fran was thinking, a bit late I thought, of "art moderne," which was all box shapes and chrome trim, wall paintings of girls with long goitered necks holding in the palms of their hands doves about to take off.

We moved when the redecorating began, to the Ritz. A hotel which never impressed me as much as it did most Americans. There was just a bit of phony class about its overpoliteness. I felt that there I was on a stage set, and the play was pretty dull; but you hoped some drama would happen. Of course the parties in some of the suites were often not the islands of decorum the hotel prided itself about. But I've heard too many stories about parties at the Ritz; I leave them to others to relate.

The Ritz, Fran insisted, was where so much gay rich American history from 1900 on was made. Its lobby, public rooms, rugs, outmoded decor suggested to me, as I walked around it— a prisoner planning his escape—a once-beautiful woman unaware she has grown old and wrinkled; who still sits proud-assed and expects the world to kiss her fingertips. It's still a posh place to the Americans and the English. To stuffed shirts, the social status seekers, rich college kids, users of the words *ritzy, whoopy, hotsy totsy.* It will be passé to those who have no Edwardian memories of tea or cocktails there, wild wild parties of the 1919-25 era, in its rooms where standing drunk in one's underwear, one could in a booze haze see the shaft of the bronze column in the Place Vendôme.

The Ritz is also a monument. "A memory album," Fran said. 15 Place Vendôme, as Napoleon looks down from his column into the bedrooms of the four-hundred-francs-a-day suites, and the maître d' gliding about like a ballet star.

Fran was pleased with the Ritz: "The place *is* old. Built in 1705 for Anne de Gramont, an old trollop and kleptomaniac."

The doorman can remember Marcel Proust, knows Coco Chanel, the Murphys and Fitzgeralds. "You just didn't *stop* at the Ritz, c'est-à-dire—once you rose to it. It's rare now that we get Americans any more who come with forty trunks. *Not* suitcases—full-sized trunks."

I used to sneak out on Fran and go down to the Boulevard des Capucines, sit at the Café de la Paix on the Place de l'Opéra like all the tired-feet tourists, and drink beer.

I was shocked to discover I had a moral sense and so strong. I was like a prisoner waiting for the moment of the jailbreak. A freedom not only from Fran, but from too much talk among the Americans of how fine a new world was being made in the old Dingo café, with Eugene and Marie Jolas, Katherine Anne Porter, Kay Boyle, Louis Bromfield, Alexander Calder. Already legend and myth were taking over. And knowing that the opéra bouffé courts of French justice, backed by the secret police of the Sûreté Nationale, kept a cell or two on the Rue des Saussaies for Americans who got out of hand: stole a bed, mocked Bastille Day or ran up debts. "Money comes before murder in French courts."

Would I miss—if I left—the Paris edition of the *Chicago Tribune*, its tout on the best bets at the Grand Prix de Paris, where a race can still be fixed and a packet made on the information?

Already the Americans who came back to Paris sighed, stood about in the bumpkin dignity of being survivors of an original group there in 1920, 1924.

"Do you remember the night when..."

The café radio had a metallic sound, and an old song:

Comme je veux je peux
Tu peux je veux
La façon que tu plaise...

One green, rainy morning when Fran slept, snoring away cheerfully like a pregnant whale, I went down to the American Express office and gave them a forwarding address: American Express, Rome. I got my money in order, went whistling "Ramona" to the right railroad station, got my stashed bag out of the baggage room. Got on the right train, sat in a first-class compartment. Soon Paris was behind me. Fran was already beginning to fade from porky-pink to gray and then soon, I was sure, to nothing. I ate a boned, skinned blue trout in the dining car, sipped only black coffee and decided I'd go back to being me as I was, not this tub of leaf lard.

Sitting after lunch, setting aside a copy of *Punch* (nothing to laugh at), I thought about myself: well, you bastard, here you go again, on your low own, after the lowest low of your low life, as Gertrude might word it.

You'll be thirty soon, you have scars and a bit of a stiff hip. At the moment you are free of clap, debt, cunt, and the gout.

You have money in your kick, a fair brain, and your interest in women is not petering out (no pun) but it is less laughing and scratching than it used to be. Sure a leg, a thigh, a tilt of the head, a thrust forward of young tits could still get you to salute at the mast. But it wasn't what it had been. Sad but true. Now in women would come the years of choice and leisure to enjoy—complacency, but no duplicity. To explore in detail what had been done in haste and youth.

You are a drunk, my friend, I said to the reflection, studying me in the window glass, beyond which glass some pregnant French cows were processing next spring's veal...You are an alcoholic, a rummy. You can't stop. You don't want to stop...Shit, I can stop any time I want...*if* I want. At dinner I only had one ball of brandy.

As a train journey continues, it settles into a progressive atrophy. The deep click of train wheels lowered their tones, and I made some notes on travel during the trip.

I travel light. I wear old slacks, repaired in the rear seam by a friend. A blue-gray shirt for day wear that needs little laundry handling. Comfortable rubber-soled shoes. A tweed belted jacket which holds passport, papers I suspect of no value, addresses, introductions I shall not present, half my money. In my pants pocket, a worn wallet with the other half of my assets. More addresses of people in Rome, Paris, London, on whom I shall not call. I also carry matches, which are taxed in Italy, a pocket comb, two old Dunhill pipes, a tobacco pouch, a key chain with keys for lost doors and luggage I don't ever lock. A fountain pen I write with, which, God and Waterman willing, should last a lifetime.

I own a fairly good-sized suitcase, it holds underwear (BVDs), two pairs of trousers, a pair of extra shoes, a half-dozen worn shirts, minor linen. I keep two good white shirts for evening wear, add two ties, a pack of light paper for a journal I sometimes write in.

I faced Europe carrying no baggage I didn't need, no dull reading matter to put me to sleep. I have two volumes of Pepys. If the toothpaste holds out, I'm set. I avoid life's wilder dramas, and expect no ecstasy. Travel, as I see it, is not to rush and thrust oneself like a jackass too far forward. There is the expectation that travel will cause transformation of one's cockeyed vision. In some a hope to achieve higher, better things merely by gazing at the best of the past—up to one's ass in masterworks. Me, I hope only the food will not make me sick. Am I asking too little? Well, I'm not Oliver Twist.

La commedia è finita

A Cold Spring

The spring of 1928 was cold in Rome. The public buildings and statues covered in spots with the shit of centuries, tobacco-brown sacred stuff no one dared to remove. I wanted to be alone, no one in my bed, no one talking in the night or elbowing me out of sleep in the mornings. I got a room in an alley behind the Piazza Navona in a building smelling of cats, living and dead cats. The room had one feeble light bulb, a bed that had a depression in its middle, and one chair. I liked it. The bath, an ancient national treasure down the hall, I shared with American schoolteachers with large dry teeth, English travelers carrying sponge bags, and a cheerful little Japanese who said "gee wiz" instead of "ah-so." He had spent some years in San Francisco. The place smelled of fritto misto and was comfortable.

I felt a kind of tension sat on the people of Rome; the lazy dago lands and quaint alleys that travel writers put down were still, it appeared, feeling the hand of Big Chin the dictator. But it was only a hint of troubles to come for everybody who didn't kowtow to the blackshirts. Perhaps they still ruined men with castor oil, and bodies were left in alleys by the arm-saluting bullies. I can't say the visitors saw much of this. There were still pasta and bambinos and young men who loitered and offered themselves to the tourists of both sexes, with that dolente look. All over the city, one felt whatever the Italians did to us—they would do it smiling.

I just drifted, avoided museums, churches, galleries; after so much talk about art in Paris, one day you find out that looking at pictures can be cured. It is not the pictures that displease— it's all the art dealers, critics, art historians, rich collectors; the whores of art, Fordie called them. When you've seen them operate, the pictures begin to mean very little—they are like debauched women with spotted faces. In Italy the paintings are very dark mostly, so it is easy to avoid them.

I went walking with an Italian artist's model named Bianca, past the equestrian statue of Garibaldi, and she made some peasant crack about the horse's hard bronze balls. I laughed and threw some coins to the street kids playing the finger game morra. Bianca looked like Raphael's mistress, La Bornarina. The same big black eyes and pneumatic paps which, when she was angry or in rut, I liked to imagine rotated clockwise or counterclock to the motion of the earth on its axis. Later, Bianca and I were drinking Frascati over our dinner at Alfredo's, or was it the Cisterna? It doesn't matter. I had porchetta, she had abbacchio arrosto, the roast lamb, and I was in a good mood. I had as yet not formed a permanent ménage. Over the Asti Spumante, my hand on her leg, I was explaining to Bianca the affinity of opposites, and she said, of course, all amici, men for women, women for men, shepherds for goats. Oh, she said, the cuckoldry, bastardy, and lechery fottiamoci led to.

Walking back to my place, past the Church of Santa Cecilia, the sounds of Palestrina coming from the doorway, Bianca told me it was the Feast of Santa Cecilia, *capisce?* saint of church music. She knew, she said, because she had been to confession in the morning and been absolved and as penance had to...but never mind *that*, she said, just think, she was coming to me in a state of grace and vorrei fare una doccia. I said she had class.

I went back to keeping my journal while in Italy—so things have a better flow and detail for me about Rome. Like remembering the water in some fountains wasn't flowing; there was always something wrong with the plumbing in Rome and the giant statues of Triton and Neptune looked like scaly lepers, their stained bodies dry, the bottom of the fountain green with scum and floored with discarded cigarette packages. Two dirty kids were slipping around inside the basin hunting the coins the tourists had thrown in to make a wish. The only wish I wanted to make was that I didn't get too interested in a bouncy blonde with a Doberman pinscher, passing by.

I felt good on the Via Condotti; walked slowly toward the Piazza di Spagna, my favorite spot in Rome so far. I had been there every afternoon for a week, with the sun just right behind me, tossing just the proper kind of rays to the Spanish Steps, the Church of the Trinità dei Monti above them. Everything terra-cotta brown, the sky a cheap blue, the women in colors that fitted the mood, the men lounging shadows. I rested by the Fontana della Barcaccia, shaped like a boat; the sound and smell didn't bother me. There were flower markets all along the steps, the sellers with no look of expectancy of a sale. The too-sweet colors of already stale blossoms were subdued by the dust of the day. All around the reddish-brown houses. I don't know why it all got me, but I felt the war *was* over—just ten years later. Over for me.

I didn't give a damn if a church was used for goats or

prayer; just as long as it took up space, and I was free to pass by and know for sure the war was over.

I decided I'd delay another week in looking up John. Friends, unlike wine, often don't age too well.

I stood leaning on the cane I carried to favor my hurt hip, although I could do without it. But a cane gave me a feeling of being casual: I didn't have to carry bundles, it said. The best part was I had no need for involvement or presenting myself shiny with rapport. I was opening up to feelings long held back. The terraced gardens of the balustraded houses had palm trees, hanging vines, oleander in pots, a bit of laundry. From my spot I could see a stretch of cypress and olives. I wondered if the large palace on the right was the Villa Medici. I was too at ease, too lazy to find out. I went into a small café that smelled of salami and caffe espresso, and ordered a glass of margroux. The large woman behind the counter was eating garbanza beans soaked in garlic and tomato sauce. When I asked her if there was a phone, she said she thought it might be connected again. She pointed to the left where it hung on the spotted wall in a corner.

I looked in my notebook and asked for a number. I waited while the fat woman ate and scratched and ignored me. Flies moved slowly on to a ribbon of sticky paper hanging from the tin ceiling. Sound came from the phone and at last a man with a cigarette-charred voice: "Buon giorno."

I asked for John in poor Italian.

"Pronto." He said, no.

I asked if an American lived there and the voice said it was signor Capponi speaking. I told him who I was and he broke into English. "Ah—he mova—six mons ago. I know not where. No addressa. No…Arrivederci."

Next day I went down and asked for John at the American Express on the Piazza di Spagna. The clerk said there was no address for him. I was puzzled and decided to try Thomas

Cook on the Via Veneto. Italians sometimes confused the two and recited ribald anecdotes about Anglo-American ways.

I was right. At Thomas Cook there was an address for John. I could leave a note. They didn't give out addresses. Very proper I agreed.

Marvelous monologue at the next café table on the Via Seminario. Two Americans, one talking, one drinking. Had to make notes.

"No, it's grand meeting another American. I'm alone, my wife passed on six, seven years ago. I just take it easy, trade a little here and there, corn futures, hog bellies, wheat. My card, you ever need information on commodities. No? Of course not.

"Great trip, so far, huh? I always say go best, go first. I go first, go where I like, sit in the sun, smoke a good cigar. My son, a contractor in Chicago, almost came with me. But the daughter-in-law had a growth—nothing serious, thank God. Dr. W——, Mayo man, treated her—with him it *can't* be serious. Her brother Jack, makes money the way others make shit, one way or the other. Out in California. Runs a private sanitarium. A gold mine. I did California last year. Through the canal. Unbelievable. More people should see it—it's big. I'll tell you about California. If I were younger, I'd buy in. Still in L.A., acres to be snapped up, Cheap. Not *cheap* cheap any more, but cheap. My brother Edward done well there. Came out of the army, looked around, married an Irish nurse; what he saw *there* I don't know—all tits. Well—Eddie, he's a rich man now. Rolling in it. Got a fine old Spanish house with a swimming pool. And the house—a real home. You don't see such solid oak beams in ceilings anymore. Our old man ran a Dutch bakery in St. Louis, and his sons not doing badly at all. Next year I think I'll go to Hong Kong. My wife—she's passed on—every Sunday afternoon we'd go eat Chinese."

The Via Margutta

Four days later after my visit to Thomas Cook, the desk clerk at my hotel handed me a blue envelope.

"You bastard! Sorry you couldn't find us. We're holed up at Via Margutta 47. So drop in any time. We are not near a phone. John."

Via Margutta 47 is one of those romantic-to-look-at, miserable-to-live-in buildings of stone, rubble, clay and rotting supporting timbers that could have withstood several prolonged sieges. I entered through large splintered gates and inside there was an open shed where some sculptor had begun a statue of a male torso from a flawed bit of marble, given it up. The several doors I passed going up on the outside staircase gave off the odor of turpentine and linseed oil, so there must have been artists behind them, and rooms for what is called an avventura, an affair. John's name was chalked on a door fading into a pale pink that had once been red. I knocked, saw a scrawled note thumbtacked under the C3: "Don't knock, walk through—pass 1st courtyard turn right past hammock."

I opened the door and found myself in a roofed passage where stood a beheaded sewing machine, a dismantled motor bike, a frame used for stretching lace curtains. A row of red clay pots were lined up with dead stalks in them. Past them was a little courtyard with blooming yellow trumpet and bougain-villaea vines and under it a hammock with someone in it, a dark-haired girl in a man's shirt, barelegged under a peasant skirt. She was sitting in the hammock shelling pea pods into a pot set between her clean unshod toes. Somehow she looked just right there. Her hair was very black, her skin very white and she was—even if the word is overused—beautiful, beautiful not in the crumby polite way one says "a beautiful woman" (meaning she isn't really plain, or meaning she's better looking than most). This was a beaut; a knockout. A bit warm, sweat-ing, irked, lazily shelling peas. The soles of her bare feet, I now saw, were soiled by the dusty stone flagstones.

"Che vuloe?" she said.

"Permesso?"

"In che posso servirla? You would be John's childhood buddy?"

I said yes.

"Sit down. I'm Brook." She threw off the pea pods from her lap and offered me a long white hand with neglected finger-nails. I shook it and sat down on a backless kitchen chair facing her. Her eyes just a little mismatched, a bit wall-eyed, and the mouth wide. Spoiling, I suppose, the symmetry of the face, if you were nuts over symmetry.

"Jesu! He'll be glad to see you."

She laughed, lay back in the hammock, naked legs kicking a bit—legs smooth as an eggshell.

You knew she ate, crapped, peed, menstruated, hiccupped, farted, was marvelously a sex rabbit in bed. There isn't anything as real as her in the entire American literature. Our writers don't know women (Okay, I grant you Carrie). I also saw Brook was pregnant, not too long, just a little bulge, a tummy below the long torso. Breasts were already enlarged. I wondered if they contained milk and felt I was a crud at the low-life thought.

"John's sleeping. He's a bit hung over. We had a hell of a night. Lazzaro sold a painting to some Greek and it *was* a night. Yes, you could say it was quite a night." She rubbed her sinuses, her temples, moaned, laughed.

I held out my gift, a bottle of Strega, still wrapped in the green paper. "I brought something."

She told me John still represented some American tool company, but he expected to get fired. He was a lousy salesman and their having a baby on the way depressed him. He was selfish she said, wanted her—*only* her.

I picked up the peas still in their shells and began to snap open the pods, drop them into the pot. The hammock gave off a squawking sound where the rusting hooks met a wall—added to other hooks set into the side of the outer wall of the courtyard.

A voice from behind a closed window shutter. "Stop that goddamn rocking!"

Brook's eyes were big. She opened them wider at the voice, sat up, long legs before her, narrow toes on the flagstones to balance herself and stop the hammock moving.

"Sweet, we have company."

I heard a bedspring rattle and she looked at me, nodded.

"Kind of lonely for company—in this alley they're mostly half-assed no-spika-de-English painters—caposcuola style."

John came through the door, his torso bare, wearing a pair of too-baggy soiled cotton trousers of washed-out blue, his feet stuffed loosely into sandals. He had grown a short shaggy beard. It was like looking at a picture taken out of focus. He looked *too* old, *too* sad. Where had the feisty kid, the flier gone? Was I missing too? Was I, myself, replaced by a stranger?

John stood facing me—too thin, the dark crepe flesh under his eyes gave an unhealthy look. His smile was as it had always been, but looser.

"You made it," he said. "You made it." He put his arms around me and hugged me to him. He smelled of unaired bedding, sour wine. Christ, I nearly cried. My life, our lives, came before me like pictures they say a drowning man envisions.

After a while, having said our banalities of greeting, John picked up the bottle of Strega.

"Brook is still married to some chicken-headed major she went to Italy with after the war."

I nodded—what else could I do?

"As soon as she gets the sonofabitch to divorce her, we're getting married."

Brook patted her stomach. "Going to be a close race, sweet."

"Glasses, glasses." John was irritated, as he would be with a hangover. And was I a letdown now he'd seen me?

"I'm a little shaky. We've been here two years. I've got to get us back to the United States. I'm a fucking washout as a sales representative."

So it all came out as we drank—that's what I'm best at, listening to friends in trouble, hearing the hard luck stories. I've heard so many I can carry them on in detail myself after hearing ten words. It came down mostly in John's case to lack of money, as in most lives in disorder. Also in people a resentment of the world having so much of it—then a wariness with each other. In Brook's and John's case I didn't think they'd reached the disliking of each other stage—maybe wouldn't. Sex, too, is a problem to some, and boredom—but here it seemed money and how to get a trip home was the problem.

I sat in the hammock while the sun sank into some Etruscan gloom, and little lizards came out to taste the shells of the peas. Some place near, a couple were quarreling in one of the rooms. The woman had a shrill voice and a dirty castigating tone; he had a deep bass that ended in a sob and an oath. She talked faster, had a British upper-class accent, and he a lowdown German.

Brook said, "It's Dody and Pete, artists."

After a while he hit her and she screamed. A kid ran past the wall of the court with a fish-and-onion pizza by the smell of it. A gramophone played "A mare chiaro." It was like a genre painting and we just sat as if posing.

After a while the artists began to make love, on the floor from the sound of it, and all the while he kept asking her to forgive him, and she kept yelling, but for him to get more violent. I felt pleased to be listening to their orgasms. John and Brook were indifferent. It was clear they were used to such daily events in this place.

It was getting dusk when we left for a pasta place. The British woman and the big dumb-looking German were standing in the doorway of their studio, arms around each other, smoking cigarettes.

"Bloody weather, isn't it?" she said to us.

"Guten Abend."

The pasta place was in a cellar and the food was strong with garlic and olive oil. John drank grappa and Brook and I had a mild white wine. They were both hungry and, as we ate, a man with a ludicrous face all warts and hair played a squeeze box and sang those sentimental songs about "Torna a Sorriento" and the Bay of Naples, and they sounded just right with the pasta and the fried fish. It was an artists' hangout; there were canvases in the cubist, futurist, and caposcuola manner, and just plain bad landscapes on the wall. I stood drinks for a few of what could have been painters and writers, and one poet.

Padre del Ciel, dopo i perduti giorni
Dopo le notti vaneggiando spese...

I felt maybe I would stay in Rome for some time. It lacked the sharp corners of Paris.

Bath Water

There were little groups of Americans much like Brook and John, all over Europe. Dissatisfied with America, or their parents, or fearing the rush and the hurry back home to get rich. Others objected to holding a job that seemed to be hell on a treadmill—as if the entire country was made up of Ford assembly lines. Some exiles were hungry, some were dying of drink, disease, or going mad according to the gospel of Saint Freud. Most managed, for in money the rate of exchange still favored us. Our biggest crime was producing little magazines. Printing costs were cheap and all the publishers of these issues had as their Holy Grail, the hope of finding another Jimmy Joyce, or at least a Hemingway. There were a lot of little La Steins around. "Hers was the easiest way to write," Brook said. "You mix kindergarten basic words with a bit of Joyce and you have the stuff to feed the little magazines."

They came, they died. Elliot Paul wrote me even the best known of the avant-garde magazines like *transition* had a hard row to hoe. He was still one of its editors in Paris.

John didn't read the little magazines the way Brook and I did. He didn't write or paint or make poems, or even think of trying.

I had a bit of luck about my own way of life when I went to see the manager of the Rome offices that handled the family's plants and mills sales in Europe. The little soot-eyed Italian, Signor Serbati, told me why he had no place for John in the organization. "These Mittel Europa people we have to do the business with, you understand we slip them under the table, you understand, il danaro è fratello del danaro. We get our customers whores, we do things after the handshake that don't come easy to Americans. Oh, you are learning, but pardon, you lack the grace. However, for yourself I have an idea. The company keeps an apartment in a little hotel near the Grand. For visiting people you understand, sales meetings, once or twice a year an entertainment. It is in blank now, empty, no one in casa, so I will get you the key. You use it."

I didn't see why not; I told the manager that nature hates a void. It was a good-sized suite and I was not damn fool enough to reject it. The hotel had room service, hot water at all hours—well nearly. And a fine view down the busy street. I was losing weight, becoming less of the fatso that had run out on Fran. I was still drinking. Fact is I was drinking hard, drinking steady, drinking with a seriousness worthy of a talent for doing things whole hog. I hated rummies who were ashamed. The grappa kept me in its grip. I'd sit up nights, the street traffic below in the late hours dying down, and the sea level in the bottle sinking. There is nothing like a drunkard on his own, the homework stew-bum, the solitary lush, to batter one's self-confidence down to nothing. Drink killed more Americans settled in Europe than automobiles.

I was making good plans to fight my drinking. I was sure, given time, and place and conditions, I'd lick demon rum. All drunks have this pipe dream—I know, I've talked to them about it. It's great conversation while tying one on. But most of us never did more than sip—in Paris, in Rome, on transatlantic ships—and think how fine it will be when we'd be off the sauce. There is nothing funny about a drunk, or amusing in an alcoholic. And something nasty in Americans in Europe when loaded. Scott became a slob and a wrecker; the police had knocked him down a time or two. Ernest, never too likable to some when sober, when drinking became a kind of cruel bastard who wanted to box or kick your legs from under you—show you his muscles. There was an American businessman trying to organize a golf club in France, who went around kicking pregnant women when boozing. A respectable New York department store lady buyer sent to Paris, when totally likkered up would lift her skirt, drop her pants yelling, "A penny a fuck, two pennies a suck, around-the-world free." Then there was the State Department boss—on sherry—who went picking up North African nigger boys in the Algerian dives of Paris. Subject: classic buggery.

The most placid American drinkers in Europe that I knew were the dedicated middle-aged rummies. They didn't yell or fight, or expose their parts, make speeches to save the world or forest wild life. They just sat on their duffs in cafés or at bars and bent the elbow lifting glass after glass, then some folding up, corking out wherever they were. If they had the wherewithal, money, the barmen took good care of them, brushed them off, put them in a taxi. When I was drinking with a few of them, I'd get this crazy impression I could hear our livers hardening with a sound like chalk on a blackboard.

The placid rummy was the kind of drunk I feared of becoming. The lush in the corner with fluttering lips, shaky fingers tearing a cigarette apart, and on bad days sitting in a pool of his own pee. I decided in Rome to try the quota system. A bracer, three fingers of potent brew, on rising. Wine with a lunch, containing a Bel Paese or Pecorino cheese, half a bottle of Chianti. A cocktail or two (or three) around five. Never more than four drinks between eating some mortadella hors d'oeuvres at any party, club, or evening out. So I'd fall into bed only half swizzled, feeling it was a tiny drunk, and tomorrow I'd cut down. Tomorrow and tomorrow.

This one morning—after two parties the night before—I looked at my wrist watch, but I had forgotten to wind it. I wondered if I already had a deterioration of faculties.

The phone on the desk holding a plaster St. Francis gave the Italina ring that seemed like a pleading for attention. The voice of the hall porter said signora (a belch) was on her way up. I asked *who?* And then figured he must mean Brook. The place smelled funky and I pushed open the windows and tested my breath on a mirror. Brook had her hair tied up turban fashion in a yellow cloth and was in what I now know must have been her one passable street dress. She carried a blue bathrobe and an English sponge bag, the kind Britons carry down a thousand second-rate hotel hallways that have community bathrooms.

I said, "Hello."

"Buon giorno, sweet. Good of you to let me come up for a real lay-down soak in your bath."

I had a vague idea she had asked me yesterday at lunch if I had a private bath and a real tub, while I was eating pasta and listening to John talk. She must have asked me and I must have nodded yes without thinking.

She looked into the bathroom. "Jesu! It's real, it's marble." She turned a silver tap and clear water gushed out. "It's clear." The steam rose, "It's hot, hot, *hot*."

She put her arms around me and kissed me. I said it was all hers—with extra towels.

"*What* a crapper," she said, admiring the throned fixture with its high overhead tank, the silver chain, and the dolphin grip for pulling. "You don't know what it's like to sponge bathe in a basin, the water smelling of frogs and the outhouse; listen, John says there must be a dead horse down our three-holer, one of Caesar's."

"Breakfast?"

"Half an hour. Caffé nero, an omelette, four eggs with Bel Paese or any formaggio. Starved for some ripe cherries or plums."

The bathroom door closed and I changed my shirt and figured I'd get shaved later downstairs in the barber shop. Steam crept from under the closed door. I felt stupidly protective. It wasn't my mess: John and Brook. I owed them nothing.

I read an old edition of *Le Sport*, all about the bicycle racers, the Tour de France, the Tour du Pays-Basque, and I remembered the races around Paris, the smell of sweat and rubbing liniment. I went to the window and looked down on some over-foliaged trees and recalled the banal music about the pines of Rome. I felt lost, like a man without his shadow: I had nothing, no set of compensations here in Rome. John had Brook, with the lovely tits, her pregnancy, and I knew I was, as the Spanish say, thinking with my cojones. Below me—I later wrote in my journal— two large Americans (North) sat in a wheeled carriage (horse-drawn fiacre) and at a newspaper stall a pimply seminary student (flat hat, flapping black robe, dirty legs) read a poster advertising a circus (Circo Arcobaleno). From the direction of the Borghese Gardens wood smoke flowed upward. A knock on the door took me away from my inventory of the landscape.

"Scusi... Permesso?"

The waiter with the breakfast wagon, and I signed his slip— lifted the cover on the omelette.

"Brook! Food."

"Just a mo', sweet."

I placed two chairs. She came out of the bathroom wrapped in her robe, legs bare, hair wet and shiny. She laughed and came and hugged me. I wasn't ready for the come-on in the bath soap,

the wet hair, the rosy scrubbed skin, the whole goddamn intox-
icating essence.

I held her close—it seemed logical and a necessity—I kissed
her on the mouth. She didn't struggle, just looked at me amused
and shook her head. "Back off. No."

"Let's eat."

The caffé nero was good and black and for Italy passable.
The omelette was large, the cheeses strong. We were hungry, the
crust on the white bread with sweet butter crunched just right.
Brook ate with healthy delight, the way a girl should eat to please
her mother. She smiled from time to time, and ended up biting
into three large purple plums, their nectar running from her
mouth, down the side of her chin. I got out cigarettes and lit
up for us both, and we sat, chairs pushed back, inhaling, exhal-
ing. It was one of those moments life is so damn stingy with.

"Bella."

"Bella."

She was from Santa Barbara, she told me, or near it. Her
family once had money, and three private tennis courts behind
a big house. Her story wasn't very interesting to me as we sipped
our coffee, and she talked. You always expect to hear wonderful
things when someone lets their hair down and they talk about
themselves, really reveal themselves. But Brook had the usual
saga of the American in Europe—women's division. She had gone
to a swell Eastern girls' school, been laid by her art teacher at
fifteen. Gone to New York at nineteen. Then to Boston as copy
writer to some advertising muckamuck who got her pregnant
and then aborted, and gave her the kiss-off with yellow tea roses
at parting. She read a lot, and wanted to be a serious writer,
but the stuff was too intellectual, the editors said. She had no
gift for dialogue (said one bastard who took her to bed) so Brook
went to Europe to type for some mission, and married this prick
of a major. Ran away to Rome, met John…Yes, yes, I nodded.
That's life. She agreed that's life. "Yes, that's life, the grand prize,

the gold ring on the merry-go-round, just out of reach as you try for it, then life gives you the kick in the ass."

After this recital, she flung herself back in the chair, hair in disorder, eyes closed, naked legs crossed, the soles of her feet were pink and clean now. Her bone structure, I figured, kept her from the over-roundness of, say, a Botticelli. Yet I could picture her stepping out of a sea shell, her feet in a bed of clam sauce, grated onions, lemon juice.

She began to talk again, tell me what she wanted.

"Know what I want? A fine dull life. A stupid easy one. A striped tiger cat to put out at night. Milk bottles to take in, in the morning. Two kids, girl, boy in that order. I admit to a wide pelvis, so could deliver easy on word of command."

Pregnant women, my grandmother had once said, should be humored.

She changed the subject, her mood shifting. I said, "In Paris they drink this stuff, Pernod, the green fake absinthe. We must find a bottle for John. There was a joint near the Gare St. Lazare where it cost twelve francs."

"Poor John—he's lost his glow for Rome."

I wish I could say I did the noble thing and got her on her way without trying to lay her. But when I tried to back-walk her to the bed, she told me she liked me fine, but she was carrying John's child and was "trying to be decent." Also she could never—she said slowly—have an affair with me. There were men she said, as she dressed, she had no desire for sexually. She was sorry, and did this news mean she couldn't come again and use the bath tub? No, I said, she could come and use it, and I'd remember I wasn't—well you know—the right mixture for her.

I never have figured out this business of sexual attraction in matching parts. With a whore you buy time and her anatomy. But with other women, to some you are at the right moment the most attractive bastard in the world, steam coming out of their ears if they can't grab your prick fast enough. To others, you're the plague, a leper and they wouldn't let you kiss their pinky. I never could figure this sexual yes and no, out. I tried reading Herr Doktors Havelock Ellis and Sigmund Freud, but never found anything deep on the subject. Just das Id and das Libido.

Hard Times

I spent the afternoon walking off a hardon, savoring the shops, gazing over the Campagna, remembering Stendhal ("The charm of Italy is like being in love."). I had dinner with Signor Serbati, who represented the family's mills and plants in Italy; a too-large dinner with a too-large wife, over-sized children. Signor Serbati, a little man with a paunch, told me Perlmann, our man in Germany, was popping the firm's money at Monte, gambling, that the family machines were selling well enough. All in all, it had been a fine year and he expected to do well for both of us if God, the Pope and the Fascists remained reasonable. The graft in season cost him quindicimila cinquecento lire—he couldn't put it in English.

Dody, the English girl painter who lived near John and Brook, broke with Hans the German sadist after a real battle.

Hans came roaring home loud like a Nibelungen opera, assaulted the locked door, broke in, got to savaging Dody till pulled off by the police, to show up a few days later battered by the Fascist cops. "Wasserkopfs! Wasserkopfs!"

Hans was deported for illegally diluting olive oil—mixed with cottonseed oil. I moved in with Dody in her schoolgirl frocks. It was as simple as I set it down; it was nearly an indifferent spontaneous movement. I didn't drink less, but I didn't drink more. Not being alone, I began to sing at the pastificis where we four took our meals. After all, it was all normal. The shared bed, I said, is the adult's sandbox.

Dody had earned enough doing travel posters to put in a bathroom just at that time. She was neat, clean, and she had been trying to get rid of Hans, who had deflowered her at an October Wine Fest in Munich because he found out "my mother was a Dame of the British Empire." At first, Dody had kept him housebroken with Liederkranz and Buckling herring. He, from the first, had insisted she dress like a little schoolgirl taking candy from a stranger. That Hans was an original.

We would make love in the wide brass bed after I took off her rompers and schoolgirl straw hat. Then Dody would hurry to get her colors mixed and go to work on a painting. She responded to sexual intercourse only at moments of great excitement, like when she sold a painting, or a critic had said a fine thing about her, or she had found the most amazing gypsy funeral to paint; the burying of a Rumanian gypsy king. Then it was the old Pavlovian reaction—it had to be fucking until she relaxed and descended to normal. She used sex as a calming release, a reward to herself, a need the way some people use prayers or I punished the booze.

Once Dody had been filled, sated, after she exploded like removing a cap from a bottle of soda, she would go back to work. Until the next need for celebrating some keyed-up emotion she was a vestal virgin. Peter Pan, paintbrush in hand. She had no interest then in screwing and had a spinster's distaste for the subject. I never fully fathomed her. During her periods of celibacy, if I would so much as slap her ass or leer, she would grow haughty and cool. As she told John and Brook, "I say, what kind of a bloody sexual maniac is he?"

Before Hans deflowered her, he had locked her up in his room—she dressed in a Kate Greenaway bib—and made her paint some flower scenes. When they got to Rome, the Galleria Blondi began to sell Dody's work; she was pleased enough with the subject matter, and she did flowers as well as anyone. She did best Italian funeral wreaths; lilies, blossoms on children's coffins. There was a demand for them in Rome.

Dody was tiny; she weighed, even during the feasting season, never over a hundred pounds, well-formed, but titless, a bit too long in the tooth, her Scotch-English children's blondness complete with freckles; cool gray-brown eyes, very large. Beside Brook, who was a big well-made girl with knobs, and who looked full of healthy food (and now with child), Dody appeared, John said, "like one of those ten-year-old kids they dress in lacy frills with wide Peter Rabbit hat, give a hoop to and send out to thrill old men sitting on benches, paisan."

John in Italy called you paisan if he liked you, just as when we were boys he called you sport if he liked you.

We'd breakfast, all four, in the courtyard on panini, butter, caffé nero, Dody's orange marmalade which her mother in Kent, the Dame of the British Empire, sent her with unheeded advice. It was very bella bella all the way—the four of us close. John and I loafing, the girls bathing; grand scenes of naked women in wet towels.

John had a temporary job translating Italian labels on machinery for export—translating into English. But it would not last. He said he wasn't worrying. Brook would have her baby—some marvelous job would be offered him in America. You bet.

Brook licked the marmalade spoon and crossed her legs, and

I looked at the tendons of her ankles, and we'd hear the murmur of Rome just over the wall. Unlike most people, I knew this was a rare and wonderful moment. It was like that, a fine warm life all that summer.

John had a lot of unresolved dilemmas, but said he'd worry later. Brook was certainly pregnant and getting more so. The divorce wasn't coming through, the major was in China on a hush-hush mission.

Midday we didn't make much of a lunch; a bit of ham, a glass of vino rosso, or vino bianco, and dinner was at the pasta joint, the artists talking those goddamn tired subjects: art, money, love, fame, birth, death. John and me doing the heavy drinking. Dody veddy British, very petite, belting away the grappa. Brook taking pale Capri. I was content with Dody, with being with John again, with looking at Brook. It was the perfect drama of nothing happening and feeling good day after day.

Coming home late at night, we'd pass the French College of the Sacred Spear and Holy Nails, a noted nest of pederasts, and we'd hear the priests' and novices' wonderful singing: "Que votre nom soit sanctifié... Ne nous laissez pas succomber à la tentation..." I would translate, "Hallowed be Thy Name...lead us not into temptation."

So we'd sleep, the full heavy slumber of feeling life could run over us lightly, make us no trouble. Yet in the middle of pleasure, I'd look down on Dody and taste bile, and feel damn, damn you Nature—but I admit I didn't get too moody too often.

One day the Banca del Lavoro said I was overdrawn and would be till the next check from the family trust. We all seemed suddenly to end our period of exhilarated fun, free of exhaustion.

Brook had taken to sulking. She wasn't as yet uncomfortable with her bulge of pregnancy—still, it was pretty obvious now. I think she feared she looked like the huge Italian pregnancies all around us: giant belly out, ballooned up giantesses going by flat-footed, ungirdled, through the streets. Puffed out and round under black cloth. Others as impregnated and bloated could still skip, wash clothes, slap children, cook in the smoke of olive oil and garlic. They climbed stairs, always preceded by their personal Alp. John said, "A Mont Blanc of living matter fertilized through pleasant apertures, blessed by Pope and priest, rewarded by the state. And perhaps according to the second law of thermodynamics, spreading heat in the universe."

Brook, I saw, was new to the whole idea of birthing—was frightened by all the child-carrying Italian women, this damn mob of breeders, fertile mares unashamed in public display.

"Why don't we get Tony to help us?" John said one unpaid rent day.

I asked, "Tony?"

"Tony—he flew with us in the RAF. He's up in Milano, screwing around with some new racing car he's building."

"Tony," said Brook. "He's the Jew boy helped us out before."

I remembered Tony was always an easy touch.

"When I was sick with malaria," said John, "we needed help. Tony's well heeled. He salvaged the Great War, you know... turned all the blood, piss, agony, and steel into gold."

It seemed Tony was in junk. Beautiful rusting junk. Tanks, guns, battleships. He cut them up with cutting torches and sold the steel to the Japs, to the British, and to Rhineland steel mills. The war was not fought in vain after all. But I couldn't grudge Tony his success.

As Tony's wing commander, I was drafted to write the letter for help. Tony was at the "A" Motor Works in Milano; he had taken on the rich man's hobby of auto racing and was building a monster there, mostly to his own plans. It was not a very good letter I wrote. All the hearty crap of how was the goddamn horny flier, and did he still play the violin when he got drunk, and would he stand at attention? Would never forget the day when—That sort of hoopla. So I added, "Stop stirring the gall stones of the local corvas long enough [oh that false old-

pals, buddies together, old cocksmen touch] to come and visit
Rome *soon*...and now lend us two hundred dollars, we're in
need of eating money." There was a lot more, a revolting crock
of shit, of chum-old-pal and are you getting much these days?
Come-join-us, it-could-be-fun text.

So that's how I knew the good moment was over. The
Roman summer was passing, humid, pious with pilgrims, dusty
and brown. Brook now had a good-sized melon up front and
Dody was deep in a huge painting of some female saint's altar
covered with flowers. I was sleeping alone on the balcony on
a camp cot. I also went walking around among the American
students at a pension that housed girls from Bennington and
Vassar and Smith—visiting to catch up with the great past of
art in Italy. I wasn't yet unfaithful to Dody, just doing some window shopping. John's job ended, the one of translating labels
into English, and Tony sent us the two hundred dollars. After
we paid our bills, there was hardly anything left. It's supposed
to be fun being down and out in some strange city—and you
don't feel as hungry when your pals are in the same way. But
that's big malarkey. Being poor is bad luck.

Dody did a woodcut print and a text to earn some rent money.

> Even though the universe destroy him, man is still
> nobler than that which kills him, because he knows
> he is being killed, and the superiority which the
> universe has over him, the universe never knows.
>
> Pascal—*Pensées*

All the time—bells ringing, money not in supply, the yowl-
ing of bambinos—there was something going cockeyed wrong
between John and Brook, something that was an undertone of
discord. Like the way they'd stare at each other with silent
anger, or she'd drop a plate of food before him—as if to say,
choke on it—or he'd look up and scowl at her if he thought
we weren't watching.

I wondered if we were all too far away from home. I figured like plants, some people say, suffer in having their roots disturbed in transplanting. Dody and Brook would get into a corner of the garden and go through that women business of whispering together in shared female wrongs. Nights, Dody and I would be in bed listening to the ivory balls bouncing together in the caffé-biliardo down the street, the husky winey voices of the pool players sounding over a strain of *Trovatore* from the gramophone of the opera fiend upstairs. Twice we heard John and Brook talking loudly, but not clearly enough to make out the beef of their discontent. John's reasoned words coming out in natural tone. Brook's fast answers, crisp rebuttal, then a mean rush of temper. John's rising, harsh words. A silence. Then the weight of turning bodies on bed springs settling to try for sleep. I'd hear a last *click, click* of billiard balls, the needle scratch as the gramophone fiend ended his concert, the drip of a courtyard faucet. Christ, what else but night in a foreign city and maybe unbroken sleep.

Dody felt John was at fault. "Some men prefer to be led to bed rather than the altar. Something's wrong there. Maybe the cazzo, he doesn't want the tot, the child."

I said, "Please, let's sleep." I took Dody in my arms and kissed her brow and said it was late and we would face problems tomorrow. Capish?

Fottitura

So I was a citizen of Rome as winter came. Cold black rains, pine trees whipping about like sadists in the wind. The fountains clogged with dead leaves, summer tourists were all gone. Seminary students in their flapping crow-black, red-nosed nuns all hurrying in one snaking line under umbrellas to see a movie. It all delighted me; Roma, Rome, pagan, early Christian, Papal, Fascist. The whores had gone indoors in the Trastevere section, and charcoal fires roasted lamb. The Pope blessed a Chinese bishop. The stock market, Wall Street was a gift to mankind. I had lost all the extra weight gained in Paris.

Tony drove down Via Turin in a Duesenberg. He told us it had been made for a movie actor, Tom Mix, but he had grabbed it off. Tony looked wider than in our RAF days, but just as dark and handsome, rabbinical and talmudically sensual. I had met

several horny rabbis. Gevalt! Gevalt! He was wearing a hairy
Harris tweed suit of loose-belted English cut. Red-orange shoes
from Bond Street of a pebbled leather that John said looked
like fruit peelings. A gray silk shirt with a wide gold collar bar,
regimental tie of a regiment never on the military books.
Topped by a floppy gray-green actor's hat with the brim way
down on one side...He had brought along a basket of bottles,
tins of caviar.

The kids in the neighborhood came out in the rain to see,
probe and spit on the Duesenberg. Tony threw coins among
them and told them in a fair Italian to keep an eye on it.
"Siamo Americani!"

"Ciao!"

We decided—as he was our major creditor and all-around
pigeon—to entertain Tony in Dody's studio. It had plumbing,
a half ceiling of a glass skylight on which the rain drummed.
Outside, feet squelched by in wet shoes and indoors the charcoal fire gassed us. But we had food, drink, and talk. We really
talked.

Tony clapped his hands together. "Sonofabitch feeling good
seeing the old RAF faces again. And you're Dody? You're Brook?"

"We are, ducks, we are. And what the hell are you?"

John poured big glasses of Strega. "The richest junk man
we know."

"Scrap metal—*never* say junk."

He drank and said our Roman district smelled very much
lived in, and we'd all have dinner tomorrow with him. Either
Capriccio's or the Biblioteca del Valle. We must, he insisted, drink
Buton Vecchia Romagna with him—ride in the Duesenberg, put
our hands in his pockets and take what we wanted. Goyem were
his best friends. He kissed Dody, he kissed Brook, who began
to laugh till her side ached, and John gave her some crushed
ice to suck. It was good and it was something you couldn't plan.
A good party jells; you can't order one.

There was Tony, my RAF wing man, making gay loud noises, offering himself, his purse, his world. ("A Jew does nothing by half, only by threes and sixes.") Later I went out down to the street with him, the rain falling with a steady purr, gleaming on his car's silver hood. We stood close together in the archway over the outer courtyard, breathing in chill air and puffing out vapor, drops of water hanging on his hairy tweed jacket, afraid maybe to penetrate such expensive cloth. There's a mood in two men meeting after ten years—but I can't express it. It's above mere faggotry.

He looked at me and smiled sadly. "Christ, ten years since a damn patrol."

"You look feisty, Tony."

"Look, any momser with a tailor and a barber can look fine." He told me of his past, how he got married in 1919. "One of those Jewish princesses—pure chicken fat—fourth generation with money, not named Shirley—what else? Deborah. A member of the Reform Temple, her brothers and uncles all married to shiksas—ready in one more generation to be Episcopalians. Banks, department stores, copper mines.

"Not bad, not bad."

"Salt-of-the-earth Jews, do I have to say? Settlement houses, free matzos to immigrants, collecting etchings. Even had relatives who went down in the Titanic. The whole schmeer. Two kids. Samuel, a girl Selma."

"What tore it?"

"I was a goddamn Glitz to those German Yahudim pricks. That's poor white trash among us Yids. Even lower than a Litvok."

Three years ago they had separated, and Tony hadn't been back to the USA, was just becoming a bigger scrap metal man, building racing cars and driving them.

He shook water off his actor's hat, patted the damp fuzzy felt tenderly. "Dinner tomorrow. Good, real good to see you."

He ran out into the rain, tall, dark, handsome, the father

of two, the man who helped junk the German High Seas Fleet. A melancholiac for sure. Charming, and I felt not too badly to be borrowing money from him. The best good money comes from somebody who enjoys giving.

I stayed where I was, a wind beginning to drive the rain in toward me under the brick arch. The smell of the wet dirt, rain-soaking wood, brought back a lot of images of crazy times past; of the war, Tony's war, my war. Seeing Tony again rubbed me raw in spots—I hadn't cauterized the goddamn memories as well as I had hoped. Tony brought a kind of breeze into our lives—with just a trace of menace. What, I didn't know. It was all so good and satisfying and filling.

Tony certainly expanded the borders of our lives. We gave up eating in cheap trattorias, gave up polenta a la Turin. Tony insisted we be well fed. "Like my mother says—take a piece of fruit. Addio. Come va!" Brook at first was standoffish. "I never knew Jews very well."

Tony had a new sports racing car sent down to Rome. He'd let me drive it—slowly—but not the Duesenberg.

Elliot Paul, who was still with the magazine *transition* in Paris, wrote me that there were two bundles of the magazine in Rome, held by some distributing outlet that wasn't pushing them. Why, he wrote, didn't I pick them up and do something sensational with them in Italy—attract attention to the issue. I could keep part of the loot on any copies sold. I knew you didn't make any money on little literary magazines. The book shops that do take them in, never, in most cases, get around to paying on what they've sold. Still, I wasn't doing much of anything and I owed E. P. a favor.

I did pick up the two bundles of the magazine, found them to be the Number 14 issues of fall 1928. "An International Quarterly For Creative Experiment." We all lay around reading copies of the magazine. There was a reprint of Gertrude's *Tender Buttons*. *"Asparagus in a lean in a lean to hot…Why is a feel oyster an egg stir,"* I remember Brook reading. There was a picture of Ernest, gun in hand, fancy cap on head, ready to murder ducks, some good Stuart Davis paintings, also a lot of fancy literary dans trying to score with the language. There was a section *Why Do Americans Live in Europe?* La Stein led off with "The United States is just now the oldest country in the world, there always is an oldest country and she is it." John said he was happy to hear the USA was a she. Gertrude added, "And so it is a country the right age to have been born in and the wrong age to live in."

Tony was away in the Duesenberg so we couldn't raise a fund to give a party for the magazine. What was needed to sell the issue in Italy, I felt, was some sort of incident, some Italian literary bombshell that would attract attention, cause headlines. Maybe bring out the newsreel cameramen who were on short rations for excitement since the war. I awoke one morning and snapped my fingers. I got John aside, and I snapped my fingers again. "It's simple. We do something to excite the Italian, maybe the world press, to mention the magazine."

"What have you in mind, murder?"

"Look, that great prick, D'Annunzio, I read is going to be in Genoa for the next three days, parading, making speeches, carrying on."

"So?"

"We borrow Tony's sports racing car, it's a road model, get photographed in it, announce to the press we are delivering the first copy of the magazine in Italy to the great wop poet in person in Genoa, to be put into that museum he's preparing on the arts of Italy. He's mad for publicity, isn't modest."

John saw the point of it at once, and like me, I think he needed a few days vacation from all his problems in Rome. The D'Annunzio idea seemed a good one. The bald toothless, one-eyed little cock-of-the-walk was a national hero, had a reputation as a cocksman—a basic Italian virtue to all classes. Poet, novelist, historian, flier; he had grabbed the city of Fiume for Italy after the war and was the hero of the Black Shirts, of all young half-wits or ticklish women.

We didn't write to Tony, tell him our plans. John left a note for Brook—and this gray morning, at six, we tiptoed out and went down to the garage where Tony had his pet racing car in storage—a low small monster called "Blue Blazes." I had alerted a Pathé newsreel man in Rome of our start and scheme, and he tried to nudge the other photo services as a favor, for a few bottles of Strega. Only one other Rome-stationed reporter was there. In the garden behind the garage, John and I put on long white linen coats and wore caps with goggles strapped on them. We stood in front of Blue Blazes holding a bundle of *transitions* between us. John waved a copy. "We bring Mother Italia, home of culture, art, and love, this publication to amaze the world and educate the wise to their own ignorance."

John was crammed into the racing car and I joined him, the bundle of magazines between my legs. It was a goddamn tight fit. John shifted gears, the car stank of oil fumes, we roared out and headed for a Roman road past the Lungotevere, Aventino, and the Foro Romano. It was early and the smoky day low down, gray. I hoped it didn't rain. This sports racer had no top. John held his gloved hands on the steering wheel. "Grand, grand, north, north, once we get past the Via del Babuino."

We had planned to do the trip in two days, issuing press notices all the way. I had a pocket of prepared typed sheets, all praising the trip, the magazine's fall issue, and not forgetting D'Annunzio, to whom I had sent a telegram quoting from Dante:

> Ah, i Genovesi uomini diversi
> D'ogni costume e pien d'ogni magagna,
> Perché non siete voi del mondo spersi?

And had signed it in English: AMERICAN-COLUMBUS SOCIETY.

John cheered up to be leaving Rome—driving and singing "Pony Boy." I was sitting iron-assed holding on. Blue Blazes had hardly any springs. And pumping gas pressure—one had to keep working a pump set in the side to get the gas pressure up. At Civitavecchia I saw John was missing other cars by inches, and I knew his eyes were failing him again. He always had a kind of cockeyed double vision under strain—his old trouble that nearly kept him out of the RAF. I got him to let me take the wheel and drove to Montepescali where we had lunch and gave out statements to three nose-picking kids and four women, two of them very pregnant. Where the hell was the press? I had wired ahead. We were arrested in Siena and the judge said we were driving on a closed-off street reserved for oxen carts and carriages of noble Papal families. John made a speech about Italy and America, and gave out our prepared one-sheet press notices. We were fined fifty lire. It was a good thing I had borrowed money from Tony. It was a slow trip after that; the roads torn up, and those not torn, in very bad repair. When we saw the silver ribbon of the Arno flowing past, there was a velvet dusk and we roared into Florence smoking badly; we had run short of oil. We were rump-sprung, worn out, dusty. The Hotel Excelsior doubted we wanted to stay there, but we insisted. John said I was Woodrow Wilson's illegitimate son by Mary Pickford. I had wired for a press conference. John was in the bathtub when the two reporters—if they were reporters—arrived. I said it was a great day for art, literature, and American-Italian friendship. We took the reporters to the Buca di San Ruffillo for dinner, and we ate well, and the short fat girl and John got very drunk. I just got slightly numb. We didn't get started till near ten the next day and we had trouble finding the right motor oil. We were pleased, however, that we were able to sign Tony's name to everything, hotel, dinner, and car servicing. We followed the Arno down to Pisa in threatening weather. The Leaning Tower was hidden by fog as we turned north to Carrara. John said, "It's going to rain."

"Hell, no," I said, pumping gas pressure and taking a sip from a bottle of Chianti.

It began to drizzle—a cold wet floating-down rain—when we came to La Spezia, and I was for staying there for the night. The clouds were black over the gulf of Genoa. John pooh-poohed the idea, saying "If we miss that potta D'Annunzio, we've flopped."

I had an omelette of duck eggs in pomidoro I would rather forget about, and John tried some pasta and edible funghi and brandy, and then we drove on along the Ligurian coastline that is called the Riviera dei Fiori. I was losing courage and felt the whole damn project was already up shit creek. It was raining hard now, wet bullets, and the interior of the car was filling up. We were sopping wet and the rear left tire was fraying; sports cars of this type have no room to carry more than one spare. Also we had been buying local petrol and that, too, seemed to do the car no good. Near dark we discovered as the battery ran down, the car had no big headlights. We stopped under a ruined tower advertising a popular cow-drench for farmers. We'd have to hand-crank the damn car.

I said we'd better find shelter. John smiled and wiped the rain off his face and from the melting visor of his cap and said, "It was men like you who turned back from California in '49 when they got as far as Kentucky. Don't be a gran cazzo."

I had been pretty active with some bottles of Terre Giulia we had stocked at La Spezia. Wet, miserable, and hungry we chewed on a length of hard salami made of old goat and candle wax by the taste of it. We blew the frayed tire as we ran across some trolley car tracks on the outskirts of Genoa, but we limped on, hunting the Hotel Mediterraneo, our goal. We nearly made it, but they were digging ditches—some Big Chin's work relief project no doubt—and we ran into one hole and snapped an axle. John and I climbed out of the tilted car and I picked up the bundle of magazines wrapped in a raincoat. I stopped a boy on a bike and asked for the hotel and he pointed and pedaled off as if he had seen the devil. We were sure messed up. Crumpled, wet, wrinkled, our caps melting, our white linen dusters all stained with the ink or dye which ran off the covers of the magazines, and we had rubbed our faces with stained fingers, so we must have looked like Indians on the warpath. Also we were pretty loaded on Italian alcohol.

I said, "I give up."

"Too late, we've already sacrificed Tony's car."

We kept telling each other how funny everything was. It helped lift our sodden spirits.

We got to the hotel and went into the lobby and they offered to throw us out. It was my turn to say John was the illegitimate son of W. W. and M. P.

They said there was a dinner in progress honoring a hero of modern Italy. I said that's our boy. I got out coins and began to pass them around. We did manage to get into the grand ballroom, guarded by two waiters who had been ordered to keep an eye on people like us. John was collapsing but I was determined. We pushed forward to the front, and I'm a little vague about this part as I had picked up a cold on the mad trip and was sneezing and coughing and wiping my eyes. But the hero up there wasn't D'Annunzio. I remember John somehow getting to a front table and dropping wet and runny copies around and leaning over—come sta—and kissing the bald head of the man who wasn't D'Annunzio. Bene, grazie, e lei. He—the man—sprang up as if stung and he and John engaged in some kind of talk in fast Italian; the hero—a stout red-faced fellow—his Italian the faster. Then we were arrested—Buona sera, buona notte!

For no reason, I was laughing hysterically. But I was so tired I fell asleep in the cell on a smelly yellow blanket. John was reciting some lines D'Annunzio had written for Eleonora Duse before he exposed their love in his book The Flame. I still remember them:

A mezzo il giorno
Sul mare Etrusco
Pallido verdicante
Come il...

We wired Tony for bail in the morning, but it wasn't needed. Somebody had pointed out to the Fascists we were Americans, and touring Italy to report how great a nation it had become.

John and I had a three-day wait while they fixed the car. John renamed it Rompicoglioni—Balls Breaker.

We drove back to Rome feeling low. Tony was angry, cursed the repair costs of the car. But Brook said, "Tony, sweet, it's only tin and rubber," so he said "shit," and took us out to dinner. You can always exploit Jewish generosity.

He refused, however, to pay a lot of the extra bills we had run up in his name. John and I were dunned by shabby lawyers, soft-looking men in worn shoes who cried real tears on the doorstep and beat with legal papers on their own brows. In time, Tony took pity on us, as there was talk of jail, and he settled everything for a lump sum. D'Annunzio heard of what had happened—and sent us a picture of himself standing on the bridge of a real battleship he had erected in his garden, signed: "La dove ho mio cuore notte e di. D'Annunzio."

Tony didn't leave after his sports car was repaired. John, after the excitement of the trip, became again the glum person he had been before the journey. He had really opened up on the trip, and it was like it had been in the war and before that when we were boys. But now he was sullen, low deep blue. Unshaved, his shoulders hunched, sucking on a cigarette butt, coughing, smoke in one eye. He and Brook were sniping each other. They were saying those acid things to each other in private that burns the skin right off a couple who still live together but are sandpapering their nerve ends to each other till blood flows. She was gelding him—he was flogging her with the idea she was just a man-trap and was knocked up to trap him.

It is the dirty low of man-woman living at such a point. I also sensed a feeling that Tony and Brook had become more than friends while we were on the trip. Desperate women, unfairly treated, turn to someone else. I doubted there had been any *fottiamoci*, actual fucking, but I wasn't sure and I didn't want to find out. Never step between two express trains, I told Dody as we got into bed—forces rushing at each other with full boilers of steam. If John had failed Brook in some way, it was clear he was under the pressures of a baby coming, no job, no money. Also Brook was still the major's wife and John had this puritan streak of morality up his spine. Maybe it was his minister father coming through in him, I don't know, but he did feel she was another man's wife. The poor bastard felt guilt.

A Winter Story

L iving with Dody became a routine—as it always does when I'm living with a woman. In the morning our rooms smelled of the ever-present charcoal gas, cold sweating walls. We piled on more of the clothes we wore, rag on rag, jacket on sweater, coat on jacket, muffler on that, looking like funny homemade store dummies. The stones of Rome rang like bells when boot-heels hit them, and the damn bells rang as always from nearly five hundred churches, calling the coughing, hawking faithful to morning mass. Again ringing at noon, afternoon, and for the last prayer of the day Brook felt the evening clang of bronze was the saddest hour of any divine mystery.

Brook grew larger, but not yet so large that she became ungainly. I doubted if she would. To warm up we'd go visit Tony as sleet rattled on the windows of his suite at the Hassler Hotel.

We'd no sooner get there than Brook would disappear into the gold-and-white bathroom to float, she said, *forever* in the pink-veined marble tub.

Dody rubbed her red nose and sat by the hissing radiator. "It's like living in depressing Manchester, this ruddy weather." Tony handed to John and me each an expensive Dutch cigar and we sat smoking.

"Why don't you pottas go back to the USA?"

John said, "If I get a job offer yes—after the kid is born."

Tony tapped the table before him, reached to shake off his cigar ash, then decided to let it fall to the rug. Dody warmed into life by the steam heat, frowned. "Not for me, the Americas."

John yelled at the bathroom door, "Damn it, Brook, you've boiled enough, get your cul out of there. We're going home."

Tony looked at me and then looked away. "She'll catch cold leaving here overheated, with that cold sleet outside."

John said, "We'll take a taxi... Brook, get out of that bath."

Tony said, "She's getting heavy, she may slip in the tub."

"Keep your Jew mind off her."

I saw Tony get ready to fight, but the bathroom door opened and Brook came out, a pile of blue-black hair done up high. She was getting heavy around the belly as the bulging robe showed.

"Stop howling and I'll dress."

Tony just stood—his hands made into two fists.

In the street John was like what my grandfather used to call "a bear with a sore ear." In the taxi, Brook bundled up against the cold that seeped through the loose doors of the rattletrap machine, just sat and stared at John.

She looked at him over the two mufflers I had wound around her neck. "You can go to hell, John."

Dody asked, "Can't you two keep it down till you get home?"

Brook said, "We'll have plenty left."

I didn't add to the conversation.

John said, "Goddamn everything."

Brook shouted in Italian for the taxi driver to stop. There was a screech of brakes, and before we could react, Brook opened the door as the taxi stopped rolling and ran off through a market area and was lost among stalls lit by flares. Night was really black in the cold street, but the sleet had stopped.

Dody shouted, "Go after her. There's ice on the walks."

"She wants to walk, let her walk."

"You filthy perishing bastards."

Dody got out of the taxi and ran toward a group of charcoal braziers where women, muffled to the ears, were gutting giant blue fish. I started to follow, but John pulled on my arm. "Dody will find her. All this because I called a Jew a Jew."

"Tony just wants to help us."

"And act the hero before Brook. He makes me look like a horse's ass. And I'm in enough of a bind already. You know that."

"I think you don't want Brook to get a divorce, or to marry her."

He looked at me with lots of hatred. And I knew our friendship was near snapping, and I didn't want that. I added, "I'm only guessing."

I could see the poor bastard was sorry for everything. It was clear it was all too much for him. No job. A pregnant girl, and living on Tony. Deep down John was not a Jew-hater.

He gave me a small smile. "All right, paisan, let's go find her."

We told the taxi to wait, and went into the market area among gutted sheep, sides of pork, split-open fish life, lobsters, all crisp and icy looking. Dody and Brook were inside a small glass booth on wheels drinking caffé espresso in the steam of cooking sprats. Being eyed by men in earth-soiled clothes, eating huge sandwiches, and drinking grappa. Brook sipped the hot brew and remained poker-faced.

John put his arm on her shoulder. "Sorry I acted like a shit to Tony."

Dody handed me a cup of espresso; we both among the four of us knew it was not at all right. Somehow we did not seem to be able to resolve the contradictions of our own natures. Outside, bits of paper were scattering before the wind, a dog drifted by avoiding the puddles. Rome in winter.

I grew to admire Brook facing her problems. Like so many women in love, she had opened herself emotionally to a man, with no reservations, holding nothing back. Now reality was crowding in and she was beginning to see John as one who had not committed himself all the way. He had loved her, desired her near him, enjoyed and been enjoyed. But when the crunch came—the test—he was a different man. The good easy times were over. The girl had become a problem, a burden—and there would be a kid. Yes, John was failing Brook, and she knew it. Her only defense was to become a bitch, a scold, and here she had no talent. Bitchiness, bickering was not natural to her. She irritated, but could not wound deeply.

The winter in Rome continued bleak; icy rains, poor heat from charcoal and little stoves. The breath we left as we walked along the streets, floating as vapor. Nights we four clung together in our (separate) beds, sharing body warmth with the partner. Looking at each other with that shivery dread of solitude if separated.

There is of course something of a worrying sensibility about living with a woman when it is not in one's own home, when marriage is not part of it. Even when there is no guilt of a society to say this is not holy, not legal; some whisper in you cannot lose all of the other morality. Free living outside of social approval is a form of true companionship. Outlaw partners can make it warm, more intimate, trembly at times because it could end tomorrow, break up. It usually does.

Then comes the dangerous thought in the night... Keep it—better marry, and own this being properly by book and holy writ, by civil decree. Only one can't own anybody, the morning says.

I took to thinking over my relationship with Dody. What did I know beyond the body, the tart tongue? Dody hardly revealed herself much when sober. She could, however, express herself well when a bit looped. It was the release of alcohol, just as making love relaxed her tensions. Fornication, I decided (too damn seriously), is also a medicine taken at regular intervals.

Walking together late at night from a café, Dody would be rubbing her nose, cheeks, and brow against my jacket. The streets empty and only a little color remained from all the past crazy centuries of Rome's history of blood, glory, prayers, and gourmet orgies. At home I added charcoal to our little stove. Dody relaxed, released after solid love making, sated, fell asleep. It was a deeper dark, the church bells in a late hour clanging. I lay on my side playing with two fingers the piano scales g, d, a, e, b, f on Dody's ribs. There was that male vanity in satisfying a woman. Something tremendously satisfying about it—almost a perversion approved of when used for healing a crisis. I lay thinking...I could open up a clinic for most of the troubles of mankind produced by the pressures of the world. I was amused, I planned a book, *The Four-Letter Cure.* "Very beneficial and pleasant advice on four legs in a bed. Feel your way to mental health. Touch contentment, reality, learn biology the fun way. Full series of advanced classes." The best thing about projects planned in the night: You *don't* write them down.

Wide-Eyed and Bushy-Tailed

Rome on Ice

Brook didn't get pneumonia or pleurisy from that Roman winter. She didn't slip on icy sidewalks. Just that during a coal shortage, she began to stain in the middle of the night. The Italian doctor I rousted out of a double bed and rushed to Brook's side said it was nothing, nothing at all. Vorrei, just for her to stay in bed and not get up till he told her. Si. Dody made soup and John brought in food from the pasta place. And we waited. Brook looked very pale, worried, and rather wonderful in the brass bed, saying she didn't want to be any bother and what a rotten way to replenish the race. The staining stopped, but Brook's bladder didn't seem to function properly. At the end of the week I insisted we take her to an English-speaking doctor from the Salvator Mundi International Hospital, which had American-trained staff members who believed in germs and clean hands and other scientific myths.

Doctor Charles V—— was young and not too sure of himself—Boston out of Johns Hopkins—but he fell in love with Brook and was serious about it. You'd see it in the way he played with his horn-rimmed glasses as he told John, "If the staining doesn't come back, I don't see anything to fear. But your wife is anemic."

"She isn't my wife," John said to the doctor.

"Oh? She's still a pregnant woman. I'll prescribe something to build up her red blood corpuscles. Liver should also help, not too well done. Yes, lots of liver."

"It's all right—I mean, doctor, the baby? Not hurting her?"

"Lying neatly in the proper position. Rather large." The doctor measured off space—as if describing a fish.

As for myself, I could already smell diapers boiling on the stove. I decided come spring, come the baby, I'd leave.

I took to walking by myself while Dody painted. To me winter is mean and yet invigorating. Like I remember January is for stables full of my grandfather's horses, where their strength is wintered—stalled. But you're aware of the animal strength. A solitary winter day I like—it's a total sort of happiness for me, the crisp coldness.

Tony was away in Milano for a few days—something had gone fearfully scientifically wrong with the casting of the motor block of his newest racer in work. I walked in a Rome rimmed in frost, saw the gray ruffled surface of the Arno—freezing people burning trash under bridges, their wet misery running from weathered noses, bodies bundled up. Walking too were lines of priests, nuns, seminary students bent against the wind. Even the bells sounding so cold as if one more ring would shatter their frozen bronze like glass.

I thought of something I had read as I walked:

Quant'e bella giovinezza
Che si fugge tuttavia.

How beautiful is youth,
Youth forever fleeting...

I was thirty-one; old enough. I had better go home. Get the
hell out of Europe. All this while walking toward the Piazza of
St. Peter's, avoiding the pigeons that had fallen frozen from the
eaves, their zeal not keeping their toes warm. The passersby
were banging their feet against the hard rock stone walk of the
Bernini colonnade to keep circulation going. The dome of
Michelangelo Buonarroti looked like a frosty bowl of pudding.
The chipped saints all along the roof seemed to shiver in the
cold wind.

There was always some droning of Latin in the interior of
St. Peter's, the basilica and the golden apse looking as vulgar
as ever, which made it more human. I enjoyed everything over-
ornate; that Catholic vanity that they had captured the only
true dogma. Too rich, too real maybe for the simple Jesus who
would be amused, I thought, at what had happened to his few
good words. After the world has knocked at your ass a few
times, you know that to bring into being what we want is the
hardest miracle.

I didn't linger in the stale old priest-and-candle smell, but
went around to the Sistine Chapel where I had made friends
with a little monk who controlled a side door; I usually slipped
him a small flask of grappa or some cakes called "nuns-thighs."
He was a fine drunkard. The little monk let me in, his breath
smoking. I slipped him the flask. He said grazie per la tua country.

The chapel and its paintings made me think of the artist,
an unhappy bastard, greedy for money, boys' culs, horrified at
his acts of sin, frightened of death, angry at popes, a patsy for
his grasping relatives. A genius given to prayer with the dried-up
cunt Vittoria Colonna; that pious bitch who almost got him

to hate living, be ashamed of his balls. On his back up there, four years painting the ceiling, screaming his rage at the work. Well, all was gone: rages, boys, greed. Left were the designs, the marbles, the great cracked ceiling. *Why* was I so thoughtful? Because I had been drinking a half dozen brandies against the cold. I began to mutter. I'm cold and hot, the casso could paint, he didn't crap out with the dice handed to him. Not to fear; rotting in his unchanged underwear. O Dio, we're all fottuti. I'm going to get away from here—from people with problems. I was really drunk.

Walking back, I went past the stalls where they sell the holy junk to tourists and pilgrims, boarded up now. On a windy corner two short Italians stood, backs to the near gale—carrying on some sly deal, their rigid hands inside their worn overcoats as they haggled.

"Forse domani."

"Io non posso."

"Forse aspetti."

Two bearded old priests, smelling of artichokes cooked in oil, passed on bicycles, toothless old men, varicose veins on their blue cold legs under their robes, carrying, I saw, the little bag, the bell, the holy unguent, to go build a salad of ash and oil on some dying person's brow, the last rites...Chi lo sa? I can't breathe—the death rattle is on me. I didn't need a brandy, but I'd have one anyway.

Into the café where the faggots hang out, flaunting their culs in tight pants, smoking cigarettes in long paper holders, running slim hands over heads of marvelously marcelled hair, adjusting their crotch for comfort. Whispering to me: "Venga venga hey Joe suchyocasso, fottere yo?" The bitches never give up and they are protected by the state like rare game birds. For there are, in season, respectable American, British tourists who can't dare get it at home, and come over for a bit of sport here. To take back the taste of it to the respectable other life. American novelists,

British poets, international playwrights. I wonder why I've never been tempted. Maybe I've smelled too many gym lockers in high school.

"Cosi, cosi."

Another day out walking I go past Alfredo's trattoria where the gross feeders are at work with over-filled plates, shovelling it in, winding it around forks, sipping it up from spoons, soaking it up in a good crust of bread. I was not hungry, just thirsty. They washing it all down with white wine, red wine, imported beer, the Strega. Faces, bodies I figured already marked for jaundice and dropsy, failing hearts, kidneys, livers; sweaty with the effort of eating, reaching for the bread, the sauces. Sighing, grunting, belching, farting. Man, I told the barman, man is made to eat, to dissolve in acid the tissues, organs, flesh of lesser breeds. See the slob tear a whole limb off a chicken (what teeth). The fat lady watching the waiter as if at a sacred rite debone the trout. I study the feeders and drink brandy—all bags of fermenting juices. I tell the barman I can, I admit to him, turn on my X-ray eyes, see their glands spurting bile into their gorged stomachs, the acids attacking the fragments of cooked animals among surgeon's scars, the colon twitching, the kidneys at work shifting, washing out the mineral wealth, the damn impurities, drop by drop beginning to fill the bladders with rich yellow piss. All the grinding, pressing, coiling, shit-making is so clear to me. Then for them only a little rest, because in a few hours they must do it all over again. Repack the guts, evacuate, overcharge the blood pressure, the glands... The barman suggests I get a taxi—I am drinking too much he says. I am. I turn off my X-ray, move outside, watch some wet-nosed children slide on an icy sidewalk that dips past trees that are only black stalks now. Kids, I tell myself, that will in their time-bind become eaters and feeders. Go now, sleep it off.

Tony's monster of a car was in front of the house. It was too late and too cold for any of the young hoodlums to be out

crawling over it, blackmailing a protection racket. I went in.
Tony, all alone, was sitting by Dody's little glowing fireplace. He
looked as if someone had been feeding him a bad oyster. His
eyes did a prowling search over my face, but didn't focus.

"It's Brook," he said. "She's in the Mundi International.
She's had a miscarriage."

"Oh Christ."

"Dody is with her. And John. I came back to pack some
things for her."

"She's all right?"

"How the hell can we know? They think so. Pretty messy.
She was pretty far along."

Tony shook himself as if to clear his head. He offered me
a cigar. I shook my head. He lit his carefully, the easy horse's-ass
way of an expert smoker, rotating the blunt end, not charring
it. He waved out the match. He wasn't showing off—he didn't
know he had done it.

I said, "You have a letch for Brook?"

"We're not all dogs sniffing around a bit of potta."

"Bullshit."

That was the end of that brilliant conversation, and we
went to the hospital to see Brook, finding her flushed and
asleep.

There's Always Rent and Death

John's and Dody's landlady, Luigini, or manager of the place—
it was hard to find out what she was—was old, and had little
of her hip joints left, and was ailing. She lived in a kind of underground den by the entrance of the place, behind pots of dead
shrubs. She claimed to have been a dancer in her youth. La Scala,
on tour with Eleonora Duse, been kept by dukes. She wore an
orange-red wig, a black dress never changed, smelled like a lobster pot, and kept asking for the rent from time to time, and
instead taking a drink offered her—shrugging her shoulders at
the hope we should get money soon. Brook asked her about
all the lovers she had when young and Luigini just answered
"Una buona parte—a good many."

Like most reformed rakes or sinners who fear their time to
die is near and the grave feels close, she was very pious and there

was always a fat unshaved monk or a dark serious priest sitting in her hovel, in their two hands a big mug of what passed for coffee. She was hung with holy medals, rosaries, and in her den the only light seemed to come from little pots of lit olive oil under lots of saints being sawed apart, fried, having vital parts removed. Under these pictures always burned the little glasses of oil; smoking wicks making the air thick and nasty.

"Next week, out you all go, if I live that long." Luigini added that Purgatory waited for all us heretics.

I decided to go back to guiding Americans around to see the sights. I had a friendship with a baggage clerk at the Hassler up above the Spanish Steps, and for a share of my fee (the bastard demanded half) he got me trade. The Americans were decent sorts and I didn't suggest whorehouses or obscene sex shows, blue movies. Old Roman stone and public buildings with sacred merde was best for them and their Brownies.

I got along great with Chuck and Alice. They ran a small advertising agency in the Middle West, were just facing middle age but not admitting it. Both trim, nice color, showing what breakfast cereals and a dull life can do for one's health. Chuck was balding, Alice's hair a popular mink color. They were last abroad six years ago when Chuck showed Alice all the places where he had shot craps in the Great War. He had been a supply captain.

They had this urgency to capture the scene that is Rome. Alice was a cow-college graduate, Chuck mostly self-educated, I figured. He was the salesman of the firm, "the contact man," as he told me, "the estimator and expert on layout, type, and format." Alice was the copywriter and a fair sort of black-and-white graphic artist as her sketch book showed. They had two children away at school, seemed fond of each other, but respectful rather than still in love. How the hell could you not like such nice people? (I wished there was a better word than *nice*.)

Chuck used to play semipro baseball, sponsored by a beer

company. Alice had a neat face, figure—by nature she was hard, crisp. Like some American wives that brought their husbands to Europe.

At the hotel bar Chuck let go a bit of his wound-up feelings.

"Why this crazy trip? What's left to do? What the hell. Alice said let's try it. Why not? Ten, fifteen years more for me and it's daisy-pushing. Twenty years more, if I'm unlucky enough to become a dirty old man leaning on a cane. I look around from when I was a kid in the north woods working with loggers as a saw-filer, and I'm suddenly fifty-two years old (tell the barman two more). It's scary when you think what you set out to do when a young punk—you know—lift the world by the short hair. And then you see what you've done so far. Not that it hasn't been worth it, hell no—Alice, the kids, the business, the way the community sees us. But at night I wake up—my pump racing— I got a murmur—and it's all like it's gone and finished. Christ, let's not see any more churches today…Got something else to see?"

I said maybe some low-life puppet show of knights and evil spirits?"

"Forget it, make it a department store."

At least Luigini gets some rent money—she was in bed in her den. "I'll be dead before you Protestants pay me what's due."

The best money I made was from a returning Italian from Newark.

"Ever eat a real beef tomato in the summer? Eat one hot from the sun with a fistful of salt to sprinkle on it? Geez—what a taste, grow millions of 'em, tomatoes." He pronounced it "ter-maters." "But we don't grow tasty tomatoes no more. Just early ripening crap—small-sized, no taste, hard fruit. The market, see, wants 'em fast, and the canners don't care what slop they put out in them fancy cans."

We were watching the traffic, seated in a café.

"No more big tasty beef tomatoes?" I asked Anthony P——, tomato grower from Newark.

"Naw. The crap crops handle easy, ship better. I should be looking after our Mexican fields right now. I got me five thousand acres in lease down there. We don't grow nothin' up north no more."

"The land cost drive you out of Long Island?"

"Hell, no. The mob big shots own New York, Long Island, New Jersey, the waterfront warehouses, trucking, produce routes. Booze, beer aren't enough for 'em. They tried to knock over my old man when he wouldn't let 'em cut in on us. So my old man, he retired. But me and my brother, Joey, we began to lease acres in Florida and ship the stuff north, only the pickers down there, the rednecks, would rather make moonshine, fuck their sisters, than work. By the time we brung in out-a-state pickers, land got too valuable for tomatoes. The Florida land boom was up our ass by 1925. So we're in Mexico now, and moving on to the West Indies. I should be there right now. Them Mexican city politicians take big graft; you gotta watch 'em."

"What the hell you doing in Rome?"

"My grandmother. See it's her ninety-two-year birthday—how you like that? Ninety-two—in Stresa on Lago Maggiore. And a cousin of mine, Mario—some chicken-raiser jerk—is getting married in Spezia. So the old lady writes to me. I'm the oldest of the American side—I gotta come over and represent the family. Among us P——'s the oldest one alive, is still boss. And she's ninety-two—still got her marbles, believe you me. Runs the olive groves, the goats, at ninety-two—gives the family orders. So I'm here, drivin' up to see her tomorrow. I don't even speak Italian. I was born in Flatbush, in Brooklyn. I'm married to a Polack girl from Newark, and my kids go to high school. I'm as much a wop as Calvin Coolidge."

"You also hate pasta?"

"Listen, you want a good pasta, the real stuff, with a sauce that takes ten hours for it to cook up? You come visit us. See what a Polack girl turned Italian, can womp up."

I said *if* I was ever in Newark...an event I hoped never to come true. As a boy I had known Newark.

All my work was for nothing. When I got back from a day's guide duty, Dody told me Luigini was dead, really dead. "The relatives are screaming their loss and carrying out everything in the place."

We, of course, all went to the funeral service at the church around the corner. It seemed only fair, Dody said, with all we owed her. It was a middle-class burial party gathered on our street. First was the most snazzy hearse, dark green with age and verdigris. Once been a burial coach, the driver told us, pulled by four horses, but was now motorized—a big dark fancy ship with plate glass sides, the frame carved with all the crazy Halloween details of skulls and crosses. Religious images in pain, flowers, lots of saints and holy landscapes. All black and polished with death messages in Latin of how fast it comes to all—no favorites. On the four sides of the coach were large silver shapes that were oil or candle lamps and from which hung fluffy black plumes and yards of black net flowing loose and tied in fancy bows like, John said, "hanging nooses." A strange-shaped casket (strange to us), wedge-shaped, was pushed into the hearse, crushing a great big mess of flowers, shoved by a crew of professional mourners (or, Dody suspected, undertakers in training), who wore gray gloves and claw-hammer coats. We stood among the mourners, watching, joining in, crying out, "Dio vi benedica!" Brook said Luigini would have loved it and added, "I don't mean it as putting it down, the whole show is good—comforting."

There was the violin-like sobbing of women dressed in soot black, veils swatching black lumps of hats set on heads. This mourning groaning grew to a wailing cry as the women collected in groups and held each other up as they sobbed, "Peccato, peccato." We saw the kids, also in black, as they wept or silently stared. The men, over-shaved, yet swarthy—all claimed to be nephews and uncles—stood in their cheap-cut black, wore black armbands, and just waited, expressionless, and spat politely. The hearse rolled off under a delayed rain that came clattering over the rooftops, the hearse creaking like a ship at sea, and the apprentice undertakers ran after it, hurling flowers on to its top as if pelting a bride. A priest muttered Latin, and pulling up his skirts, hopped into a following car. Three other cars were packing with sobbing people. A fat man coming up late, waved an unfurled umbrella at a passing taxi, while a few overlooked mourners stood waiting with worried faces for more transportation, stepping on the flowers underfoot. There were no more cars.

John said, "Goodbye, Luigini." We all felt a sort of true feeling of death here, agony let loose in sobs and wails at this *final* parting from a relative. Not like the American burial racket, Brook said, "Some indifferent Holy Joe or rabbit to talk up the merits of the dear departed—mostly all lies—someone most likely he had never met."

We had to admit how much more tragic and true to living and dying the Italian death scene was, how closely the relatives felt the loss that was carried off in that bouncing macabre boat on wheels. To a rented grave—the bones to be turned out in twenty years. Just how horrible death is—an Italian funeral gives it to you like a hard punch in the face.

The D.T.s at Midnight

S cientists, all the nosy medical crowd, might be interested
in my delirium tremens, the D.T. attack. If it were up to
me I would just as well have skipped it. Certainly I've never read
or heard anything like my midnight attack, as to details. I had
been drinking hard in Rome, but I had been drinking hard a
long time. It was more than a habit with me—by then it was
a tradition. I had been drinking everything I could think of, and
when I went once a month to collect the funds that came to
me from the United States, I had a habit of visiting a few bars,
beginning with one on the Via Condotti near the place where
I turned my check into lira. I could go for continual drinking
for several days, drifting around the Via Sistina, Via Veneto, if
I was in a weak mood. Just drinking with strangers, newspaper
men of all nations, a visiting American or Englishman. So almost

without knowing it, I was taking on a lot of drink. Holding it—as the saying is—very well, well, fairly well...O Dio we're all fottuti. He has us by the cul and will not let go.

So this night, after a bad day with the grappa and a new brandy, I'm in bed more or less fuddled. Having somehow gotten hold of, and brought home, a bottle of Polish slivovitz. Dody was away late at some art show opening. John and Brook had gone to see a new French film in the Piazza Duomo. I came to from sleep, or a fainting fit, feeling as if a large firecracker had just gone off in my stomach, and I saw the walls of the studio, painted yellow, turning brown before my eyes. Aging. Even I was growing old, turning brown fast. My hands shrivelled up, covered with liver spots. The bones of my skull were trying to thrust their way through my paper-thin skin.

I knew I screamed. I think I yelled for the waiter to bring a caffé espresso. Everything in the world was in the process of decay. The newspaper on the table, as I watched, was turning brown, into dust. The fruit in the wooden bowl was rotting, I could see the big pretty peach turn from pink to umber, to sepia, wrinkle to soft foaming rot, then it became only a dry pit that split open—there was no kernel—*that* scare-buggered me—no kernel? The wooden bowl itself was being bored through and through by worms, and the oak wood dusting away.

I screamed again and couldn't grab the slivovitz, just knocked it off the table. The timber rafters, solid walnut, overhead, began to sag and crack with age and turn to sawdust that fell like snow. I yelled, didn't the fools know, didn't the horses' butts see *everything* in the world had suddenly aged, died, crumbled, decayed, fallen apart? The very stones in the street were cracking, splitting as rain and cold seeped into them. Young girls were turning to hags at an alarming rate. Virile well-hung males were becoming creepy old men swinging ball bags containing no kernels of anything. Nothing was dreamlike, nothing hazy or out of focus. I want to make that point. Everything was in sharp detail.

It was a dandy attack—flames searing my guts. I kept howling and thinking too, clearly, thinking in all this crazy agony *why* didn't I see pink elephants, little blue men, snakes? That was the ticket for D.T.s...all the D.T. cases I had heard of, you had to have snakes. I was being swindled out of snakes. Big slimy ones, cold coiling snakes, slithering reptiles. Yes, I felt cheated, even now when the earth was very old and man-made walls gone. Chi lo sa? I was lying on earth, modern Rome was one hell of a mess, what was left of it. Just a pile of junk, rocks, dead cats, old shoes, matching the broken stones in the Forum. As I kept screaming, the sun began to grow dimmer, lost its heat; that snatch-hunter, H. G. Wells, was right, I yelled. The sun was dying, the earth on which I lay would freeze, or was I wrong? Wasn't the sun due to explode and burn everything into fireplace ashes? The earth—poor bitch—I saw was a big lump of a clinker, burned used-up coal. Everything, everybody gone to become burnt-out match ends. So why was I still screaming, why was I left when the rest of the earth had aged in a few minutes, stopped existing? What should have taken a few billion shitty years had come about too early. My pain was tearing me apart—I was in labor giving birth to a Sopwith Camel.

Then hands came out of some place, grabbed me. I tried to howl and couldn't. Tried to spew up all the fire, everything inside me, and didn't.

There was this big bastard of a turning wheel which seemed made of old rags, and it spun faster and faster over my head, going like a sonofabitch and it was making me very dizzy. All the time my heart seemed to be playing with its regular beat—was skipping beats, adding beats.

There were the faces again of Dody and John and this Italian fellow with the whiskers, who looked like a waiter in a trattoria I knew. He was in a white coat and he was holding a drinking glass out to me with a bent glass tube; and telling me to drink, and I did. It was a dreadful brew—smelled like the stuff they scrub toilets with. I could see I was in a strange room with cracks in the ceiling and walls of pale green—one small barred window with a gray day outside.

I couldn't hear anything—I mean to make logical sense of— even if John was talking and Dody gabbing away and gesturing too. I just seemed to have lost my stomach and my lungs, and mice were gnawing at my rectum, biting and tickling...Then I fell away into a black bag, came to in a colder new room. There was a kind of a coastal sea mist in it. I was wrapped in a light very wet sheet. My arms were strapped together. A gush of ice cold water hit me. I tried to scream again. No dice, maybe I did, but I heard nothing. I was lying in a dark slate tub, like a black marble coffin, and a tap out of sight was filling the tub with ice water, and I couldn't move or get air to yell shut it off you pottas! Someplace an overflow drain was carrying off some of the water, and the tap was keeping up the choking flow right up to my chin, my head on a kind of stone pillow.

How do you die? I kept thinking: they say it's easy. Not for me. It went on hours, this cold, cold bath. Then I was on a table in a wet sheet and I was sipping something sick-making from a glass tube, with a tar taste. I couldn't puke it up—just brought up some cottony foam.

A fat Italian with gold-rimmed teeth and a wedge of black moustache, slapped my chest and asked was I awake? Good, good. Quant'e bella giovinezza. He wore an undershirt only and soiled gray pants and had tattooing on his biceps; on the right one, Christ on a cross, on the left one, the Virgin. I went black again as I tried to see what he had tattooed around his collar bone. All the time I was feeling so ill I could not understand why I lived. I was weak and sick as a skinned-alive cat. I don't remember the days, but I was someplace south of Rome,

the tattooed man told me, in an international drunk cure farm.
There were two other shaky American patients, a few Germans
with rum-blossom noses, the rest I didn't try to make out. We
read old magazines, sipped bland soup, peed with such shaky
fingers at fly buttons we spattered ourselves. We walked around
on worn linoleum in ratty slippers covered with lint, wore blue
terrycloth robes. We didn't talk much. Young wop studs in
white coats, with too-broad shoulders, kind of pushed us away
from the front doors and barred sunroom windows. They'd
give us a nice hard pat on the chest to get us to sit down—and
stood by smiling when we drank more of the fearful tar brew.
If we didn't toe the line, we were stripped and wrapped in a wet
sheet and *bang!* into the slate tub and the ice water for a few
hours. After a while you toe the line and get half a cigarette
reward after each meal. They light you up. You own nothing.

There was a chess set and checkers with several of the red
ones missing, a deck of cards swollen twice their thickness by
greasy overuse. Somebody was always hoping to start a game.
A piano stood in one corner of the sun room, its yellow keys
were badly cracked—like untreated cavities. A tall man with a
bad cheek tic tried to play on it once, picking out a few notes,
and gave up.

I was only at the drunk cure farm nineteen days, Brook
told me, when Tony picked me up in the Duesenberg and took
me back to Dody's studio.

"You were, luv, really tearing the ruddy world apart," Dody
said, while I sat scared to move in a chair, and felt the need of
a drink. I was what was known in the drunk trade as dried out,
but not cured. I don't know any lush who ever really gave up
the craving. Even if some became non-drinkers and were so goddamn smug about it when they tut-tutted you lifting a glass.
Some place these characters—non-drinking boozers—months
or years later you'd find them in a relapse—hanging one on, or
on a hell of a bender.

I had some Frascati wine with lunch, one glass. Dody put it to me plain. "You'll taper off, darling, or out on your arse."

That seemed fair.

John was a little kinder, but a bit of a puritan—I was so weak I just sat, and I heard a lot of crap about what friends were for; for standing by in times like these, and I could make it, for I had character I learned. Tony didn't say anything cheering—just patted my back and asked did I remember the wartime flying, and living off milk and brandy—vomiting it up all over the cockpit in a tight corner? I said I did—thank you, Tony, and we're all in a tight corner, aren't we? After that, they left me alone.

I watched my drinking and didn't stand too close to cheerful tourists in bars on the Corso Vittorio Emanuele, or strike up cozy with too many gossiping loafers in cafés. I didn't want the horrors again, just wanted enough to get a nice edge. I seemed all raw inside and I had a sinus condition, most likely gotten from the damn freezing ice baths. I never did clear that condition up completely. Even now, at night, one or the other of my nostrils closes up and I awake, my mouth bone dry, sucking air through a mouth and throat made of leather.

I tried not to think of the D.T. attack, but it was always on the back burner of my mind. I kept my boozing just below an imaginary red line. Once above the line, I knew, back would come the end of the earth through sudden and rapid aging, the death of all living things but me, the end of the sun. Everything, everybody incinerated. I didn't want to do that. I had friends who were entitled to their lives, I told myself after the third Strega. Good friends and I'd keep the earth green and inhabited. All the time I was very frightened and very taut. Also I was sure I'd never survive another treatment on that drunk farm.

A Simple Solution

R ereading the journal I kept at the time, I see I had been trying to explain the hold that Brook had on most people who knew her. Even a powerful attachment she turned on in those who were close to her. She herself did damn little to encourage such feelings. She seemed good, lazy, placid, bitchy, kind, in turn. With a sort of tender penetration to the nerve-ends inside you. Hell—I know that's not a subtle way to put it. But so how to put it? Tony said it was some cock-eyed sensibility. I settled for her intense luminous stare that made her either Mona Lisa or a mental case. She was neither.

In the hospital room, after her miscarriage, for some minor female infection, she half sat against a pile of pillows, looking paler than the paleness I remembered. Her black hair loose and flowing around her head ("I'm thinking of bobbing it"), I sensed a deadly tiredness in the relaxed body, emptied, the baby gone. She, under the sheets and a blanket tucked so tight around her, was still attractive. I decided she was not in herself anything mystic, she was a reality, not an ideal. And I just sat and had silly thoughts like that—me too convalescing. She wet her lips with her tongue.

"Where's John?"

"Sleeping in the visitor's room on a couch. First time he has come in three days."

"The baby is dead. Maybe he's blue about it."

"Wasn't really a baby yet. A kind of fish. No, I'm lying. It was a baby. I could feel it kick."

She moved her head to look past the hothouse flowers, too bright in their plain glass vase, past the gifts of crackers and packed fruits, all sent by Tony—to the long narrow window and beyond at the gray day, but as yet no rain.

"Hand me the barley water."

I gave her a glass of some pale whitish drink and a bent glass tube. She sucked on it and I took back the glass and put it down. Just below the window, white campagna had once dragged marble for the Farnese Palace. I remembered an old print of the scene.

I said, "What goes from here on?"

"Good question."

I nodded. I said, "Come back to America with me."

"Don't be a dope."

"Tony?"

She closed her eyes and made a thin line of her lips. "I feel hollow. First I must heal, then think. Then act."

I made an easy gesture of yeah-do-that, and took up a pear from a basket. I wondered if she was running a temperature. She, Brook, was irritable, confused, angry too—all of which was understandable. Women have a lousy set up about sex in our society; then, too, their plumbing is often emotional and their

fertility a problem when all one partner—usually the stud—
wants is fun and games. I don't know if nature planned it that
way. But it is a dirty trick. Brook had been bruised, fingered,
cut, sewed, had bled, felt dizziness, nausea. And what else in
her aborting womb? She'd been drugged, humiliated by enema
and bedpan, packed, handled. So I wanted her to gripe.

She held out a white hand and I took it, pressed it finger
by finger. She said, "Take John home. And send in the nurse.
I need the bedpan."

John was sleeping on a too-short sofa in the visitor's room.
Tony was smoking a short English pipe and reading a month-
old copy of the *Paris Herald*. Dody was knitting something that
never seemed to take final shape. Tony asked, how is she? I said
she was peeing.

I suppose a novelist would be able to fill in what I can't—all
kinds of arty dreck about love and sacrifice, only I never knew
this business of men and women to be like in a novel. Not in
any novel I ever read...Tony and Brook, the first good clear
spring day in Rome with a sun trying hard to warm old stone—
the two of them went off together in the simplest way possible.
She stood in a neat yellow silk suit, hatless, short shingled hair,
and told John she was leaving him, and he said he had known
for some time she was. We were just about to start breakfast in
the garden. John said he had not gotten over loving her, but
he had lost feeling deeply about things. He said he wasn't sure
it was that simple. But he had nothing to offer her and she was
her own boss. Dody just poured coffee and I put jam on bread.
John said he didn't feel any pain yet, but he didn't touch his
eggs and bacon.

Later he told me he hadn't driven her off. It was he, himself, who moved away. He didn't know Brook, he said. "You go
sleep with a girl and you play all the crazy things you can think
of in bed. Okay? Okay. But all the time you're not going to get
to her, to herself. You follow what I'm saying? No matter how

deep you penetrate. And you don't think she knows what you are, either. It's so goddamn sad it's that way. After a while it comes around to accepting what there is, and then..." He made a gesture, palm up. I wasn't going to give him any buddy-in-trouble advice. I had been in his spot a couple of times. Never, of course, with anything as fine as Brook. I suppose I'm a man who will take up with second best in everything but drink and food.

As to Tony, he was pretty stiff about the situation. He acted like he knew he was a shit, and yet at the same time doing something that was best for Brook. All wrapped up in love. That feeling when a man is led by his balls, when he isn't really too sane. Tony was like that as the whole thing came to its climax. Tony, lightly sweating, watching his words, and being crisp and polite, like a bad actor playing a part he didn't like.

There was a lot of new shiny luggage with heavy brass locks, smelling of the best leather. Which was a mistake. Better if Brook had left us with all she had in the world in a brown paper bag. She didn't have much of anything anyway. They had popped a lot in the pawn shops the year before. But Tony continued buying toilet things of silver and ivory, traveling clothes and shoes. I felt that showed callousness. John and I stayed away a lot the last two days. John said it wouldn't have lasted, even without the baby, and it would not last with Tony. He gave it six months: "On the outside, six months."

I said I wasn't so sure it would fail. Tony would get a divorce—Jews are very honorable about these things—and see Brook got one too. She'd settle down, married, the wife of a rich junk man, pardon me, a scrap metal dealer, have kids and become a dreadfully happy bore—flower shows, weekends with Tony's business partners, join a good temple or go Christian Science.

John nodded—said Tony would get fat and bald and his nose would grow. I said not bald, but fat anyway, we drinking leisurely, but nice and steady—getting a bit high. We didn't either of us say anything of what we really thought; something, the close glue of intimate friendship, was ended for all of us. There would be big blank spaces in us for some time. And what was sad now would be, in the future, all crusted in the crud of nostalgia.

I told John I was going back to America. The family trust and the board of directors, the nephews and uncles who ran the mills and plants, were going to give me a fresh chance to prove I could stop drinking and they would see, as the lawyer's last letter put it, about "a place for you in the organization, an organization in which so many of your family have so often proved themselves."

John went to see Tony and Brook off—they were taking a plane to London. I begged off. The day they left Rome, I was sitting in the Comparetti café near the Capitoline Museum where the Greek and Roman statues no longer appealed to me. How many times can you look at the Dying Gaul—all he needs is surgery and iodine. I waited, drinking black coffee and rum— nibbling on hothouse grapes not too well cleaned of the saw-dust they had been packed in. It was warm inside the café. I tried not to think of anything too involved. Just the world out-side: streets, cities, fields. Besides all that, there was the moving on of time present, carrying me in its mouth like a cat a kitten, into time future. Drink makes me sappy and lyrical. I couldn't go beyond that on just black coffee and rum.

John came in, tossing his hat at six feet onto the rack. I wanted to cheer him up by saying that to be betrayed at least proves we still exist, but I didn't think he could take much of my wisdom today.

He sat down and said he'd have a coffee and rum—nothing to eat. He looked at me first grimly, then with a smile of affir-mation. "That's it."

"Saw them off?"

"Wasn't it the right gesture?"

"Always thought gallant gestures were a pain in the ass."

He put his ungloved hands around the hot coffee and rum cup. "I wasn't very fair to Brook, or good to her."

"It wasn't that."

"I know. I didn't want a family, a wife."

"It must have been beautiful—the final parting. Were you sober?"

"You bastard. No drinking. Didn't want to appear crocked. Wanted to carry it off. You know, modern, flip. Didn't say it, felt like reciting...Goodbye old chap, just wanted to say hope you and my girl have a fucking good time of it. Only sensible thing to do. You love her, old chap, she loves you. You marry her. Piss on the eternal light at the tomb of the Unknown Soldier for all three of us. Pee, you know, is held sacred by Eskimos. But no, we were so civilized; you'd never see anything carried off better in a British regiment when someone steals the mess funds."

John was weeping silently. I didn't glance away. Without looking up he told the waiter to bring two Sarti brandies. I watched him drink both of them. I said he was selfish and ordered for myself.

I don't suppose either of us were men of action. The old Paris crowd I remember, when romance cracked partners got roaring wrecking drunk. Picked fights, got a dose from a casual pickup. Reacted as a romantic should. John fingered an empty glass but didn't order a fresh one.

"We're in *great* shape. Let's go home. Dody is cooking some special dish. If she can keep the turpentine out, it should be tasty."

John put his head on the table.

"Oh God. Brook, Brook."

He didn't come home with me. He said he wanted to watch the crowds, the traffic. He said he never felt alone and beat, not when there was animated life—even Italian. "I crowd in."

I let him go. I didn't want to play head-holder, back-slapper. He wasn't the kind to fight the police, or kick pregnant women. Let him cozy up to the crowd. Also I had to explain to Dody my own plans.

I was torn from sleep by John's coming home, his hard banging of doors. I could recognize his footsteps any place.

I turned and put my arms around Dody and went into a locked-in sleep which lasted till the sun woke me. I lay a long time wondering if I should wake John for breakfast.

Home is a Hatrack

The French Lines *Rochambeau* deposited me at its New York pier. I made (like a kid again) the old ride with the ghost of my grandfather; the ferry across the harbor to New Jersey, the tube train to Manhattan Transfer, then a Pennsy train south. Backward, dumped backward into time on a sooty train, the invisible smoke of my grandfather's cigar up my nose. The passing Pennsy stations—no sacred merde, just chocolate, grimy brown with wear, remembering that when I dream bad I always am on a train making that run and I'm coming back, trying to reach the town I grew up in. But, damn it, I never get home in the piled-up dreams—it's as if a huge rubber band is pulling it out of my reach.

In reality, I made it as easy as pie. The old red depot leaned just a bit more as the termites continued their work inside the

walls, the dog-wagon EATS, where I had bitten into hamburgers and gooey cakes, was still in need of paint. I motioned to
the taxi man, Artie—he had an upturned nose, no hard
bridge—he was sucking the stem of a kitchen match as he
leaned on an old Dodge with the hand-lettered sign: TAXI.

"Hello, Artie, still hacking?"

He looked up, needing a shave, his pants unpressed, his
shiny jacket food-stained, the match hung in the corner of his
mouth. We had been in high school together; he had left in the
second year to marry a plump Polish girl with cheeks like over-
ripe apples.

He said, "Wouldn't a known you. Spats, cane, the derby
hat."

"It's a bowler, not a derby."

"Looks like a fukkin derby to me."

I got in. "The old house."

L—— Street, the business section, had slipped a bit. Some
of the old buildings had new shitty facades of bad taste. New
fronts, window dummies looking as if someone was goosing
them. Boys and girls, just the kind I went to school with—same
laughter, horseplay on the sidewalks, in front of United Cigar,
Poplar Drugs, the Greek's soda joint; only they were fifteen
years younger than me with one toe in middle age. The Country Side Livery Stables were now the Hollyhock Garage, the
Dutch Reform Church, corner of F—— and N—— streets, was
gone; turned into a busy department store. THE BON TON
stood there in a too-gay contrast of yellow and red. Once-
empty lots that I had played football on held two-story buildings selling auto parts, Model-T Fords on secondhand lots,
naked white bathroom fixtures, bargains in canned corn, sliced
bacon. Fruit stands covered some sidewalks. There were two
new undertakers with signs in glossless mat black and thin
gold. NONDENOMINATIONAL. CREMATION. ORGAN
CHAPEL. (Local juoe, I bet.) On side streets I glimpsed new

red brick, rows of houses in no style known to history, with no summer porches, just flat fronts, clapboard second stories, all alike. All having thin roof wires which were radio antenna.

Upper L—— Street, the toney residential section, still had charm; large private residences, some elms untrimmed and only a bit diseased. I saw a lack of care in many of the places. A lawn in need of cutting paint peeling from the Van D— house (Regency plus Gothic), the B——'s yellow brick palace (Rhine castle and French provincial) window's boarded up, signs of fire marking the upper walls. Weeds in possession. FOR SALE. *Zoned for Business.* I felt I should feel depressed. But I was really elated coming back.

My grandfather's house looked about the same, neither smaller nor larger. I had been in fear it would look smaller, as places in your youth are supposed to shrink down when you go back. Another big lie. It was good to see it; large, old, the first part going back to 1832—and every time some generation made a bigger pot of money there were additions and improvements. It looked the same; the English box and yew hedges a bit thicker, the old oak over my bedroom window gone, lost in some storm I supposed. The porch swing still there, the chains rusted; the swing on which John, Chunky, and I had smoked my grandfather's cigars after a night of it with the factory girls and strong applejack. Sometimes we three sitting there in July storms in the rain, watching the people run for it.

I had been sent the keys and I let myself in. Every house has its own smell. No place had the same mixture of fumed oak, varnish, floor wax, cellar draft through the floor vents. The house was part of my family trust—I couldn't sell it, but I could use it or rent it. An old uncle had lived in it but had died three months before with perfect timing—as if I would have booted him out. (Maybe I would have.)

I sat in my old room that night, looking at the wallpaper that had faded down like an old Japanese print exposed to a hell of a lot of sunlight. There was the ceiling stain where I had killed a large bug with a copy of *Tarzan of the Apes*. The windowsill where I had carved a skull and bones with my first pocketknife. All around me the simple tokens of a gone world. They made me even more lost when I lay on the patchwork bedcover, shoes off, puffing on a pipe, watching the smoke rise to a shelf where there was a badly stuffed woodchuck I had processed in 1909. The Old Nostalgia had me, and I let it hold. I was a little ashamed of myself, letting myself be such a memory nut. I had to admit it tasted good.

I liked being home. It seemed solid and honest and had character; so what if maybe I was deep in some emotional gaucherie. It was like a man who respects a girl and doesn't try to get into her pants before he's sure she wants it. And never has to ask her to kiss his navel. I'd been curious and impatient about how it would be coming back. I'd soon know, and today I was tired, not in awe of the old house, no, only comfortable in it. I got a bit mumble-tongued trying to talk to some rooms, and went to bed, happy and with no plans, no plans at all. I put myself to bed in my grandfather's room in the high-backed walnut bed. Took off my shoes, opened my collar, any moment expecting to hear an old familiar voice shout down the long upper hall that the world was going to hell in a hack. I'm as sentimental a bastard as the next man—if the combination is okay.

The town didn't look too well in the morning, not from the big bay window. It had in its newer part the appearance of speculators' quick jobs. I felt I could huff and puff and blow it all down. Only I didn't. Fuck progress.

The Swenski, last of the hired girls my grandmother had trained, served me coffee, tasteless toast, spoke of my dead uncle—he was an ass pincher. The good plate of fried ham and eggs cheered me up. I almost pinched her myself, she middle-aged but with good legs.

I walked crosstown passing the new movie theatres, the Stand and Majestic; Rod LaRoque, Ronald Coleman. The Majestic also featured SIX ACTS! HI-TYPE VAUDEVILLE! Ted Healy, Hartman and his Piano, Apple Blossom Girls in Flower Time Revue, Six Yamamoto Brothers—*Jugglers Extrod!*

The police looked thinner. I sensed speakeasies behind several heavy doors. The old side streets which had ended in mud-holes were built up, overcrowded with clapboard rows of houses all alike, as yet lawnless, treeless, but already occupied by mothers and babies. I saw only one horse, pulling a Polish junk dealer's wagon from Hunkytown. Hunkytown was now a separate incorporated community called R——, Artie the taxi driver had told me. Ward heelers were courting the voters and soon public offices would be in the hands of the Poles, Irish, Hungarians, Negroes, southern crackers and rednecks that had come north during the war for high wages and stayed on to overbreed and encourage incest. And why not? My family had come in a hundred years ago to grab all they could, and they were crackerjack grabbers.

The old corner drugstore with the red and green jars was gone. A chain drug company building of blue and white stood in its place. LUNCH, MAGAZINES, PRESCRIPTIONS, CIGARS. A soda jerk was reading the *Daily Running Horse.* I knew he could tell me where to find whiskey, but I was on the wagon—proving myself to America and the family mills and plants.

Visiting one's dead is very satisfactory; they can't talk back, and it makes being alive seem very well worthwhile. The old burial ground of the family was hidden away on a good expensive hillside. It had escaped the damned fate of the more modern graveyards heavy with marble to keep the dead from rising and coming home for supper.

Among the family graves the cocoons and nets of spiders and moths were hanging from bull briar and outlaw roses gone crazy wild with thorns like barbed wire. A comfortable place, not fussy or too neat.

Leaving the taxi, I walked along a narrow path, gravel long since washed out. The fence of wooden palings painted white. Then a very black crow took off from a patch of yellow flowers. He was a lousy flier, banked too steeply and labored at his wing work. Never make the RAF.

There was the smell of fertile dirt, the hum of insects. An old pint flask, its glass become pale purple by sunlight, lay across the path. Lots of nighttime lovemaking here, I was sure. There were no great stone angels, no tormented lumps of granite or marble, no bleeding hearts, saints or putti. The early members of the family lay buried under brown stone slabs. Bastards, hotshots, faithful husbands, cheating wives, hard workers, cocksuckers, pious prudes.

I came to a mound on which wild daisies spilled yolky pollen. My grandfather and grandmother's graves. My mother and father's. The graves seemed to suggest a rest on picnic grounds rather than the lousy mess of dying. I brushed aside the vines to expose spiders who made tracks, hurrying to other darkness. There were the stones on which names and dates were cut. Also on a low border slab the text I remembered from the few Sunday School classes that I had been trapped into attending:

Shall mortal man be more just than God?
Shall a man be more pure than his Maker?

Artie came down the path to point to his watch to show that time was still being lived by.

"We could," I said to the taxi man, "go down to the river and wade barefoot."

He shook his head, "I gotta meet the trains."

I remembered when I was seven—my mother and father's bodies brought back for burial here. The undertaker didn't offer to shake hands (gray gloves, striped pants, winged collar, ascot tie slightly frayed, a smile smelling of peppermint drops—even as a kid I knew the bastard had been knocking back a few of grandfather's bourbons).

"The departed are on view in the library. This way."

"No." I never did view the dead if I could avoid it.

The Reverend K——, a kind hard-working man, wet his lips hunting for some goody in holy writ to toss at us—my grandmother sobbing. I turned away. I was not going to cry. Up till then, I had, unlike most people, had a very happy childhood. I loved my parents in a casual way. But gone is gone. I was frightened by this funeral, all the black cloth smelling of mothballs and other dead, the dying flowers, the smell of furniture polish—*that* would be the caskets in the library.

Now I was back—and childhood a million miles away. That happy childhood—and even when puberty came *that* was rather fun in a different way.

My grandfather's stone was simple. I turned on my X-ray eyes and saw him down there under the dirt and gravel: stretched out, a brown parchment package of dried skin, covered with poisonous moss. His bones protruding, the teeth (had they buried him in his best set?) grinning through the receding shrunken lips. I felt good he was so near.

I wondered if when I died would they permit me to be buried across the foot of both my grandparents' graves? Like the dog of some murderous crusader and his faithful duchess, effigies I had seen in an English church. Shows how morbid one gets on giving up drinking. Emotionally sloppy.

I sat on the graves which would, some day—sooner or later—take me under. I wondered why did not other Americans come home? Life on strange shores is usually an impiety, lazy or a quick hustle. The mind in exile doesn't act—it mostly merely condones action in others. Up yours, Europe.

I've begun to wonder, were those years so good and fine

and crazy really fun for us? I had to admit honestly—cross my
heart—that perhaps they were. It was not just nostalgia, and
not being young anymore. The twenties, going away soon, were
really alive and full of new forces, new kicks. Maybe they
weren't as important as we thought. And what we did wasn't
as good as it looked. But it was better than what may come later.

There were things I had seen, ignored, but being done and
being said, and being carved and painted, that were so new
they scared. The last of Dada and cubism, and the first of sur-
real and the hot-pants writers panting after Proust and Joyce
and Gertrude. Why Stravinsky was almost a classic. Jazz was
out of the whorehouses. I had merely brushed with small irrel-
evancies at big meanings. But what had counted most was the
living, the fucking, the drinking, and the people involved. I
hadn't played the creative game—I was background—one of the
figures in motion—but I had stumbled into some daffy advance
guard and didn't join the parade. I had just been doing what
seemed to me being alive in a screwed-up world.

So? I went down to watch the trains come in. Mostly they
just went by by by.